CAST YOUR

CARES

CAST YOUR

CARES

A 40-DAY JOURNEY TO FIND
REST FOR YOUR SOUL

DEVOTIONS FROM

ABIDE CHRISTIAN MEDITATION

WITH STEPHANIE REEVES

ZONDERVAN
BOOKS

ZONDERVAN BOOKS

Cast Your Cares
Copyright © 2022 by Carpenter's Code, Inc.

Requests for information should be addressed to:
Zondervan, *3900 Sparks Dr. SE, Grand Rapids, Michigan 49546*

Zondervan titles may be purchased in bulk for educational, business, fundraising, or sales promotional use. For information, please email SpecialMarkets@Zondervan.com.

ISBN 978-0-310-36339-2 (audio)

Library of Congress Cataloging-in-Publication Data

Names: Reeves, Stephanie, author. | Abide Christian Meditation (San Mateo, California)
Title: Cast your cares : a 40-day journey to find rest for your soul / devotions from Abide Christian Meditation. ; [Stephanie Reeves, Abide writer and content editor]
Description: Grand Rapids : Zondervan, 2021. | Includes bibliographical references. | Summary: "For those seeking peace and comfort amid the worries and stress of everyday life, Cast Your Cares by Abide Christian Meditation offers forty daily reflections that invite readers to give their concerns to God and receive Jesus's promise of peace of mind and heart with each biblical story, journal prompt, and prayer"—Provided by publisher.
Identifiers: LCCN 2021037018 (print) | LCCN 2021037019 (ebook) | ISBN 9780310363378 (hardcover) | ISBN 9780310363385 (ebook)
Subjects: LCSH: Peace of mind—Religious aspects—Christianity. | Fear—Religious aspects—Christianity. | Anxiety—Religious aspects—Christianity. | Worry—Religious aspects—Christianity.
Classification: LCC BV4908.5 .R44 2021 (print) | LCC BV4908.5 (ebook) | DDC 248.4—dc23/eng/20211006
LC record available at https://lccn.loc.gov/2021037018
LC ebook record available at https://lccn.loc.gov/2021037019

Cover design: Studio Gearbox
Cover image: Siwakorn1933 / Shutterstock
Interior design: Sara Colley

Printed in the United States of America

21 22 23 24 25 26 27 28 29 30   /LSC/   12 11 10 9 8 7 6 5 4 3 2 1

To those who help me when the burdens are heavy:

David, my husband of more than thirty years: Thanks for always having my back and sharing my burdens (even if you think you're one of the main ones!). I love you!

My kids, Justin, Nathan, and Morgan: God knew what he was doing when he gave me you guys. We're better together.

My grandson, Zayne: We didn't expect you so soon, but you came into our lives right on time. Thanks for keeping me laughing and giving me your warm, fuzzy heart.

Wonder Women: You're the best friends ever. Thanks for your enthusiastic support!

Neil (CEO of Abide) and Russ (executive producer): Thank you for believing in me and trusting me with this book.

Abide Nation: I don't know your faces and only know a few of your names, but you're the reason we do what we do at Abide. And this book was written with you in mind. May God add his blessing to each and every word you read.

And it should not go without saying that God is my very present help in times of both trouble and joy. This book is for him and because of him.

Stephanie Reeves
ABIDE WRITER AND CONTENT EDITOR

CONTENTS

Part 8: Identity

INTRODUCTION

What's causing you to not be able to rest today? Your finances? A loved one's health? Fear, anxiety, shame, loneliness? Each care can feel like a boulder set in a backpack heaped upon your shoulders, causing you to lie awake at night, unable to find rest for your body or your spirit. You may wonder if you'll ever find a way out.

Maybe the lyrics to the famous *Frozen* song performed by Idina Menzel come readily to mind: "Let it go!"

Or maybe you've seen this pithy statement: Let go and let God.

So easy, right? Just let it go.

Unfortunately, it's not so easy. Some of what's weighing us down and causing chaos digs barbs into our souls and refuses to release us, like those sticky little burrs that often cling to our pants when we walk through weeds.

Hebrews 12:1 encourages us, "Therefore, since we are surrounded by such a great cloud of witnesses, let us throw off everything that hinders and the sin that so easily entangles. And let us run with perseverance the race marked out for us."

Throw off everything that hinders.

But doesn't it feel sometimes like you're wearing a straitjacket that you can't just take off? No matter how hard you try, your cares entrap you.

The good news is that God is not asking you to do any of this on your own.

Philippians 1:6 says, "Being confident of this, that he who began a good work in you will carry it on to completion until the day of Christ Jesus."

And Jesus said in Matthew 11:29, "Take my yoke upon you and learn from me, for I am gentle and humble in heart, and you will find rest for your souls."

Everything you've ever dealt with, every emotion you've ever felt, is covered in the Bible. Anger? Check. Loneliness? Check. Shame? Check. The list goes on and on. Jesus knows exactly how you feel. That's why he wants you to spend time with him. And that's why we created the Abide app and wrote this book. We want to help you spend time with Jesus, learn from his gentleness and humbleness, and find rest for your soul.

Anxiety is still the number one mental health concern worldwide, and it's on the rise.[1] From 2020 to 2021, the percentage of adults who reported symptoms of anxiety or a depressive disorder increased from 36.4 percent to 41.5 percent.[2] And while we know there is a connection between mental health and emotional health,[3] we also know Scripture addresses and relieves each of these troubles in specific ways.

Considering how your thoughts and mindset affect your beliefs and behavior isn't new, but doing so with visualization practices based on the immediate relief available in the Bible's promises is proving the benefits of daily reflecting on Scripture in new ways.

We had one listener write to us to tell us he was a drug addict struggling in recovery. He knows the solution lies in his relationship with God and so he wrote to tell us how thankful he was for the inspiration in the meditations.

We hear stories like this all the time. People write just to tell us how much they need the content in our app. They get busy or their hearts are heavy, and they just need to remember God's love.

Sometimes we just need to be reminded that we have the greatest source of help available to us. Psalm 55:22, the verse from which we got the title of this book, says, "Cast your cares on the LORD and he will sustain you; he will never let the righteous be shaken."

Jesus really does want you to have peace, but not just any peace; *his* peace. In John 14:27 Jesus tells his disciples, "Peace I leave with you; my peace I give you. I do not give to you as the world gives. Do not let your hearts be troubled and do not be afraid."

This book goes beyond the Abide app to offer practical, biblical strategies that immediately address and help resolve eight primary "cares"—common fears and anxieties—drawn from Abide's most popular content. Through applied visualization techniques and meditation prompts, these devotions will help you put the words and instructions from Scripture into practice.

This book isn't a cure-all, and if you've had traumatic experiences, professional counseling may be warranted, but these devotions are a means of ushering you into God's presence, giving you practical steps to identify and release your cares, and prompting you to write down your thoughts, experiences, and prayers. Keep a journal by your side as you read, and don't feel like you need to go through the chapters in order. One day you may need to release your loneliness, another day, your anger, and another, your everyday concerns.

Use this book as a tool to work through your cares with God whenever you feel restless.

It is our deep desire that in forty days, by reflecting on God's Word, releasing each particular care, and journaling from the prompts given at the end of each chapter, you will find the rest your soul so desperately needs.

Stephanie Reeves
ABIDE WRITER AND CONTENT EDITOR

PART 1

ANXIETY

Seeing God in the Storms

Reflect on God's Word

Are there hurricane conditions in your heart today, leaving you feeling frightened and out of control?

Perhaps the storm that scares you is a relationship on the rocks, a child in distress, a situation at work that threatens to go badly, or something else. Whatever it is, today God invites you to remember that he is with you in the storm, and that he is in control.

Matthew 8:23–27 tells the story of Jesus on the lake with his disciples when a "furious storm" comes up.

Imagine that you are one of Jesus' disciples. You've been following him for a while, and today has been, as usual, a full day. Jesus has healed so many people, and the crowds keep following him, even when the things Jesus teaches seem confusing and hard.

What is supposed to be your time of peaceful rest on a lake is interrupted by a sudden tempest. High waves sweep over the sides of your boat, and wind and rain whip at your face, but Jesus keeps sleeping.

Finally, you go to Jesus and shake him. You say, "Lord, save us! We are going to drown!" He looks at you with compassion. "You of little faith, why are you so afraid?" he asks. You watch as he stands and speaks to the wind and the waves. Everything suddenly becomes completely calm.

Perhaps you hear God asking you the same question today that Jesus asked the disciples on the boat: "Why are you so afraid?"

Physical storms can be very frightening. Hurricanes, tornados, tropical storms, and even thunderstorms can bring great devastation. And there's nothing we can do about them but make preparations and then either evacuate or ride it out. Because of today's technology, we know when physical storms are coming, but we don't have Doppler radar for emotional or spiritual storms.

Nevertheless, Jesus wants to speak the same words to you today that he spoke to his disciples: *Don't be afraid.* Perhaps he wants to calm the storm around you, or perhaps he simply wants to calm your heart. The storms you face may seem overwhelming, but you can be sure that God's power is greater than any storm. Today, he invites you to rest with him, to trust him with your life, so that even when a storm rages, you can be at peace.

If God is for you—and God *is* for you!—you have nothing to fear. The powerful one, the creator and commander of wind and waves, wants you to be at peace in his love.

Release Your Anxiety

Take your hand and place it directly in front of your face, about an inch away. What do you see? Only your hand, right? Now take that hand and move it back about six inches. You can start to see a little more around it. Now hold your hand at arm's length. Suddenly, you see a lot more than just your hand.

Staring at your problem, the storm in your life, can take all your focus. Instead, focus on God's presence in the midst of your storm. There is nowhere that he does not dwell. Jesus was in the boat with his disciples during the storm that worried them so. But instead of focusing on his presence, and the fact that they were safe with him, they focused on the wind and the waves.

Yet Jesus showed them, and he has shown you, that he has power over all he has created. Can you trust that he has power in your life, too? Imagine Jesus turning his eyes of compassion to you. Because he loves you, you can trust him with all the fears and worries in your heart right now. Take a moment to give your fears to God.

As you inhale, feel the breath expanding into your chest. Slowly exhale, feeling the breath leave your body. Let your breath continue this way, growing deeper and steadier, as if the same calm that descended upon the lake at the sound of Jesus' voice is moving into your body with each breath. This is the life-giving oxygen that comes from God above, and it can calm your soul, settling the anxieties you may face.

Rest here for as long as you need, giving your fears over to God and receiving his love and grace. Today, if the storms of life descend suddenly upon you, remember this moment and this truth: God has power over the storm.

God, you know all about the storms swirling around me today. You know my fears and worries, my weaknesses and my needs. I surrender them all to you right now. I know that you are in control and that you are a God of power and love. I trust you, Father, to take care of me, and to calm the storms in my heart and in my life. In the precious name of your Son, amen.

JOURNAL PROMPT: Write about a storm you currently face. What would it look like if you felt God's peace in the midst of that storm?

The Practice of Casting Your Cares

Reflect on God's Word

Trying to cast your cares on God is like playing with a boomerang. You throw it as hard as you can only to have it come right back to you. That's the point with a boomerang, but it's frustrating when this happens with our cares and concerns. We want to throw them to God, and we don't want them back.

First Peter 5:7 says, "Cast all your anxiety on him because he cares for you." Just cast all the things you are worried about onto the strong shoulders of the almighty God. Sounds peaceful, relieving, and restful, doesn't it? But what does it look like? How do we practice casting our cares on him?

When we give something over to someone else to take care of, we are saying that we give over control, that this is theirs now. Our cares are gone. Off our shoulders. There's a prayer called the Serenity Prayer that asks God to grant us the serenity to accept the things we cannot change (to cast our cares on him), the courage to change the things we can (to do what we can to address the cares), and the wisdom to know the difference.

It's often this last part that causes the majority of our trouble. But we worry less when we seek God's help, asking for *his* wisdom to reveal what we might do to change or accept the situation.

So when your teenager keeps making bad decisions, you pray and ask God to help you release that child to him. And when the desire overwhelms you to constantly check where they are, or to worry about who they're with, or to question them when they get home, you take a deep breath and release that worry. They are in God's hands. Ask God to give you wisdom for how to respond to your child. Ask that he bring friends into your teen's life who will influence them to make better choices, who will build them up rather than tear them down. You might have to do this over and over again, but keep turning your worry over to God. As you do, his peace will fill your heart.

Or maybe you're concerned about an aging parent's health. Perhaps you see them struggling with memory issues or the ability to take care of themselves. Even as you might make decisions to get them the care they need, you find yourself burdened by the load of your care. And so you pray and give that care into the hands of not only *your* heavenly Father but also *their* heavenly Father. Each time the knot of worry pulls tightly on your stomach, take a deep breath and remind yourself of how much their heavenly Father cares for them. The burden is not yours to carry.

Quite frankly, we can't take care of everything by ourselves. We were never meant to do that. Instead, our loving

God desires us to come to him with all our shattered dreams, disillusionment, dashed hopes, and fears. He waits for us.

Remember that what feels like such turmoil within you doesn't even stir the waters of God's great love for you. Your anxieties don't faze him.

Because God is so big and so powerful, those concerns aren't too heavy for him. Let God have them because he cares for you. Remember, he knows the future, including *your* future, and his plans for you are good. Cast those cares.

Release Your Anxiety

Take a few minutes now and ask the Holy Spirit to remove any barriers within you that keep you from coming to God with all your cares, all your worries, and all your concerns.

Now imagine yourself sitting on a dock, fishing pole in hand. Visualize putting your cares, worries, and anxieties on the end of a fishing line and then casting it out onto a calm lake. What do you put on the end of your line? Finances? Relationships? Health? The state of the world? Picture tossing the line far away from you. Feel and hear the line spin out of the reel. Watch as it drifts away over the calm water.

Imagine those cares, worries, and anxieties on the line drifting into the hands of God. Picture him removing them from the line and sending the line back to you with the gift of peace attached, reminding you that he is now in control of those fears and worries.

Take a few moments now to thank God for taking your

cares and handling them so you don't have to worry about them anymore.

> Creator God, the world around me tells me different-
> ly, but please help me remember with every beat of
> my heart that you are more than capable of handling
> both my cares and the causes, and you give grace to
> the humble. Help me take off my mask, the mask that
> says I can handle everything myself. You know my
> scars under my mask. You know my vision is obscured.
> So help me to come to you and learn from your hu-
> mility. I offer and pray this in the name of Jesus, your
> Son, our Savior, and my Lord, amen.

JOURNAL PROMPT: Write down the worries that you struggle to surrender to God. Why do you think you hang on to them so tightly? Could it be pride? Fear? The need to be in control? Could it be that you feel threatened? Ask God to help you loosen your grip on them now.

Trust . . . Then Act

Reflect on God's Word

Picture in your mind the story that's told in Exodus 14, the story of the miracle God did to save the Israelites from Pharaoh's army. They were at the edge of the Red Sea, water lapping at their toes, and the Egyptians were coming fast behind them.

Can you imagine being there, departing Egypt with Moses? You're carrying everything you own on your back. Your feet are blistered, and sweat drips down your face. You wipe your forehead and look behind you, and then you see them: the Egyptians, in the distance, their horses pounding toward you, throwing up clouds of dust.

The people around you begin to cry out to Moses: "Was it because there were no graves in Egypt that you brought us to the desert to die?" And you wonder the same thing. Were you wrong to trust Moses—to trust God? Was this all just a trick? But Moses lifts his staff, and the crowd quiets. "Do not be afraid," he says. "Stand firm and you will see the deliverance the LORD will bring you today" (Exodus 14:13).

You are terrified! Stand firm? You and everyone around you just wants to run as fast as they can. And then God gives these reassuring words to Moses to tell the people: "The LORD will fight for you" (Exodus 14:14).

Can you feel peace beginning to settle in you?

That internal peace strengthens you, and it's a good thing, because now God calls you to act, to move. God says to Moses, "Why are you crying out to me? Tell the Israelites to move on. Raise your staff and stretch out your hand over the sea to divide the water so that the Israelites can go through the sea on dry ground" (vv. 15–16). Moses moves to the front of the crowd and raises his staff over the water at the edge of the sea.

And then the miracle happens: This huge body of water, the mighty flowing Red Sea, a barrier that there was no way to cross, suddenly splits in two. But you realize that God is not going to pick you up and carry you across. You have to move. You have to put one foot in front of the other. As you take that first step, you marvel at the dry ground beneath your feet. It's not even muddy. Friends walk on both sides of you, and you can smell the salt from the water and feel a light spray as the wind blows. It's refreshing. Just like trusting God.

Just as he called the Israelites, God is calling you to step out in faith.

The Israelites were afraid as the Egyptians chased them. They were afraid they'd be killed or taken back into slavery. Those were legitimate fears. There was an army at their backs and a sea in front of them. You might not experience the hot breath of an army at your back, but your fears can feel like one.

But think about how you have seen the Lord fight on your behalf in the past. First you needed to keep silent and to remain calm. To wait and to trust. To see how God would deliver you. And then you needed to move. You needed to do whatever it was he told you to do.

Release Your Anxiety

Today, practice being silent and still, and see what God will do in your silence and stillness. Trust him to make a way and then to walk with you in it.

Maybe your chasing army is an unhealthy home situation that you really need to leave. But the Red Sea of your finances faces you. You see no way around it. So you keep waiting for God's provision, lamenting that you are stuck. But are you limiting God in how you expect him to provide? Miracles can come out of unexpected places. So as you pray, ask God to help you to see what you're not seeing. What steps might he be asking you to take that are scary to you, but that you need to take while holding his hand?

Perhaps quiet and stillness feel unfamiliar. Perhaps you feel a need to fix the situation you're in yourself, or to worry your way out of it. That never works, does it? When you try to fight your battles on your own, you often end up feeling the weight of the struggle in your body. Your neck muscles become tense, and you may experience headaches, fatigue, or even illness due to stress.

So slow down. Focus. Take a deep breath and shake off any distractions or worries. If they try to return, tell them they can wait. For now, you are resting in the quiet; you are breathing in God's goodness and exhaling away those distractions.

You can rest here. God will carry your burdens. God will help you fight your battles. Let your breathing grow deep and slow as you turn your focus to the God who fights for you.

Take time to declare your trust to God. Tell God, "I believe you will deliver me." Then listen for what he's asking you to do.

Rest in this quiet place for as long as you need to, knowing you can trust God to make a way for you in every circumstance.

Dear heavenly Father, soften my heart right now. Remind me that my salvation doesn't come from working hard or doing something to earn it, but that my salvation comes from you. Teach me to sit still in your presence, and to know when to act, when to wait, and how to trust. Thank you for your love for me. Thank you for delivering me from my sins and promising me abundant life in Christ. Thank you for sending the Holy Spirit to dwell in me forever so I am never alone and am always connected to you. Help me to trust in you alone, and to wait for you in silence and stillness. And when it's time for me to act, help me to act with courage and to step out in faith. I pray this in Jesus' name, amen.

JOURNAL PROMPT: How does your anxiety keep you from being able to trust God to make a way for you and then walk with you in it? Write down some ways you may be seeing God provide for you that you didn't notice before.

God's Waiting Room

Reflect on God's Word

God often makes us wait, even when we're praying fervently. Abraham and Sarah had to wait until they were in their nineties to have a child (Genesis 17). Joseph spent many years in prison before he became a leader, second-in-command under Pharaoh in Egypt (Genesis 40–41). Job waited through devastation for the Lord's restoration (Job 42:10). Simeon waited most of his life to see the Messiah (Luke 2:25–35).

In Psalm 27:14, David encourages those of us who wait. He says, "Wait for the LORD; be strong and take heart and wait for the LORD."

Why does God ask us to be strong and take heart while we wait for him? Perhaps it is because he tunes our hearts and strengthens our character in the waiting. When we rush in and try to take matters into our own hands, we can miss what God has for us in the waiting. When we are faithful and trust that God will work, we practice patience and grow strong.

The Amplified Bible enhances the meaning of "wait" to "confidently expect." How does waiting differ from confidently expecting the Lord? Take a moment and think about what currently requires you to wait on God. Are you simply waiting, or are you *confidently expecting* him? Consider how changing your focus to expectation would feel.

"Confident expectation" can also be translated as "trust," something we see in a story found in Mark 11:12–26. Jesus had just entered Jerusalem on Palm Sunday. He and his disciples spent that first night in Bethany. Early the next morning, as they were riding back into Jerusalem, they passed a fig tree. Jesus was hoping for something to eat, but he found the tree didn't have any fruit on it, so he cursed it, saying, "May no one ever eat fruit from you again." The very next morning when the disciples were walking by the same fig tree, it was now withered away to its roots. They were shocked.

Imagine the scene. You are next to Jesus with his disciples that second morning. Just like them, you are shocked to see that what Jesus said to the tree actually happened. No one would ever eat the fruit of that tree again. You hear Jesus say, "Have faith in God. . . . Truly I tell you, if anyone says to this mountain, 'Go, throw yourself into the sea,' and does not doubt in their heart but believes that what they say will happen, it will be done for them. Therefore I tell you, whatever you ask for in prayer, believe that you have received it, and it will be yours" (Mark 11:22–24).

Do not doubt. Trust. Trust that God is good and is watching over you and caring for you. The most important prayer we can pray is that we would know God for who he is, no matter how he chooses to answer all our other requests.

ANXIETY

But some people want to believe that Jesus' words mean that God will give us whatever we want. But we only have to look at Jesus to see that this isn't true.

Not long after the incident with the fig tree, Jesus was praying in the garden of Gethsemane. Knowing that he was about to be arrested, wrongly convicted, and crucified, he told the disciples, "My soul is overwhelmed with sorrow to the point of death" (Mark 14:34) and went off to pray alone. He prayed, "*Abba*, Father, . . . everything is possible for you. Take this cup from me. Yet not what I will, but what you will" (Mark 14:36). Jesus was "deeply distressed and troubled" (v. 33), and yet he aligned his will with God's will.

We need to do the same. How would wanting what God wants change your prayer life?

Not what I will but what you will. Not an easy prayer to pray, but when you know God is good, it's a lot easier to let your will be aligned with his.

Release Your Anxiety

Are you waiting for something today? Maybe you're experiencing acute anxiety over a situation that feels out of control, and you feel as if God isn't doing anything about it. Jesus urges you to trust in God's goodness.

Praying may sometimes feel as if you're just talking to the ceiling. So take a few moments and remember those times when you heard from God. Hang on to those times. Remember that your feelings at the moment have little to do with the reality of God's presence. He is *always* with you, and he *always* hears your prayers. But his answers aren't always what you expect, or even what you want.

You may hear a clear yes, or you may hear a clear no, but sometimes God just asks you to wait and to listen and to open your heart to a transformation that Jesus wants to bring into your life.

So stop today and wait. He is here. Wait with a heart open to him.

God, you work all things for good because you are goodness itself. You do all things in your perfect timing, and you can use waiting to change me into a more patient and peaceful person. Right now, I give my anxiety over my circumstances to you. Take my anxiety, take my impatience. Instead, give me peace. Let me trust you with my whole heart, holding nothing back. Strengthen my heart and give me courage to wait with patience. Lift up my heart to live on your time and not mine. In Jesus' name, amen.

JOURNAL PROMPT: How would you describe the difference between waiting, expecting, and believing? How does your focus change when you move from waiting to confidently expecting?

The Landscape of Your Life

Reflect on God's Word

When you imagine your future, perhaps you see loneliness, like a barren desert. Or perhaps when you picture the future, it's full of work and responsibilities, like a city street with bumper-to-bumper traffic.

King David, in Psalm 37:3, invites you to envision a different future: "Trust in the LORD and do good; dwell in the land and enjoy safe pasture."

This goes beyond the "bloom where you are planted" bumper-sticker theology. God had given the Israelites a land and had proved his faithfulness to them over and over. No matter where they were, God was always with them. He was there in their wilderness wanderings, and he was there in the promised land. The consistent factor? God's presence.

When the original spies were sent out into the promised land in Numbers 13, their report was mixed: Sure, the land bore amazing fruit, but there were walled cities and . . . giants! Caleb and Joshua alone were ready to take them on. But the people grumbled and cried against Moses and Aaron. The result of their grumbling was that they were not allowed to enter the land.

King David asks you to put down roots in the land God has given you, to dwell in it. *Dwell* is a word that suggests something that lasts, not something temporary. We are to settle in, to make ourselves at home, and then rest in the safety of God's faithfulness. We work, but God is also working on our behalf. We see the Lord's face instead of the weeds of loneliness. We rest in his faithfulness and love instead of wrestling with fear of relational famine.

We see this same truth in Philippians 2:12–13. The apostle Paul writes, "Therefore, my dear friends, as you have always obeyed—not only in my presence, but now much more in my absence—continue to work out your salvation with fear and trembling, for it is God who works in you to will and to act in order to fulfill his good purpose." We are to do good and dwell in the land; but it is not our work that ensures our security; rather, it is God who feeds us with his faithfulness. Like sheep with a good shepherd, we trust him to care for us. Whether we have few friends or many, a job we love or one that simply pays the bills, God is our provider.

When you trust in God, your perspective of the landscape of your life changes. Even if your actual circumstances remain the same, your trust in a good God to provide for you changes the way you walk through life. The mental traffic of work and worry can subside, and you can breathe again.

Maybe you've just moved to a new city. You don't know anybody, and your attempts to connect with people at your new job have fallen flat. All you can see in front of you are months spent in your lonely apartment. But God is there.

Maybe he is asking you to get up on a Sunday morning and check out a church down the road. Or perhaps he is opening up opportunities to volunteer with kids or invite in international students. When you see the possibilities for planting a harvest, even the desert may suddenly bloom.

Imagine a future that looks like safe green fields instead of back alleys with danger around every corner. The truth is, not only will God be with you in your unknown future, but he is already there. He knows what's coming. He doesn't want you to be afraid.

Release Your Anxiety

Today, consider what it might look like for you to trust in the Lord. How can you choose to do good and to dwell in the land?

Pause for a moment to reflect upon God's faithfulness to you. God invites you to trust in him and to learn how to dwell in the land he's given you. Ask God to show you the good you can do.

Take a moment to check in with your body. Are there points of tension or stress anywhere? As you breathe in deeply, let that breath go straight to the points of stress, and then exhale the tension.

Continue that slow, deep breathing. Breathe in healing breaths to the tight places in your body and exhale tension and stress.

Take a look at the landscape of your life now. Perhaps it is filled with craggy mountains. Maybe it's dry like a desert or crowded with too many buildings. Consider that this is the land God has given you. As you look around you, can you see evidence of that?

It's easy to be anxious about your future, but sometimes that anxiety focuses on the present. What mountain overwhelms your current landscape? Picture God holding your hand as you scale that mountain, or see his awesome power as he pushes it aside. Can you trust him either way?

What desert do you feel you're currently living in? Maybe you feel your relationship with God is dry, or you can't see through a financial crisis that's draining you. Picture God providing oases along the way, small pools of water to give you relief. What have those moments of relief felt like? Picture God right by your side through it all.

What are the skyscrapers that loom over you? Too much on your to-do list? Too many people demanding something from you? Too many responsibilities? Take a deep breath, hold it a moment, and then release it slowly. Ask God to show you which buildings can be torn down and replaced with life-giving gardens. What can be set aside because it's not yours to do?

Stay here with God, if you can, until you've heard what he wants to tell you about your life, about where you are now, and about what is ahead for you. Put your trust in this good God to provide for all your needs as you follow him.

Father, today I want to practice trusting in you. Help me to obey your commands and to learn to be faithful. Help me to understand what it means to dwell in the land you've given me. Give me eyes that can see my life rightly and a heart that trusts you completely. Thank you for your loving provision. Thank you for meeting me in my current landscape. Thank you for teaching me to obey you, to practice kindness, and to cultivate what you've given me. Thank you for promising to provide for me faithfully. In Jesus' name, amen.

JOURNAL PROMPT: Talk to God about the landscape of your life. Describe any place where you feel God isn't, any corner where he doesn't dwell. Why do you feel that way? How can you remind yourself that even in these places, he is with you?

PART 2

LIES

God's Promises Are True

Reflect on God's Word

When God told King David what he planned to do for him in 2 Samuel 7, it must have seemed too good to be true. God promised to make David's name great, and to give Israel a safe home. God promised that he would establish his kingdom forever through David's descendants.

David responded to God's promises with humility and faith. "Who am I, Sovereign LORD, and what is my family, that you have brought me this far?" he prayed (2 Samuel 7:18). He praised God for his faithfulness, and declared, "Sovereign LORD, you are God! Your covenant is trustworthy, and you have promised these good things to your servant" (2 Samuel 7:28).

God made promises to David, and he kept those promises. He did make David's name great. People would sing of him, "Saul has slain his thousands, and David his tens of thousands" (1 Samuel 18:7). God gave the nation of Israel a safe home in the promised land. David's kingdom was established forever, as the line of the Messiah came through him. But that didn't mean David's life was easy. David did not always have victory. He experienced loss and heartache. He lost an infant son and an adult son who had rebelled against him. He lost many warriors in battle. He faced the chastisement of the Lord because of his sin. And still he trusted God's promises.

God has made promises to you, and he will keep his promises even if you are unfaithful to him. God's faithfulness is not dependent on your performance. God is faithful because God is God. It is his nature to be faithful. But God does not promise that your life will be painless or easy either. It can be tempting to think that God is not keeping up his end of the bargain when life gets hard. But generation after generation after generation has proven his faithfulness.

Let's look at some of those promises.

In James 1:5, God promises to give us wisdom if we ask for it with faith. "If any of you lacks wisdom, you should ask God, who gives generously to all without finding fault, and it will be given to you." Think of one area in your life where you need wisdom now. God uses his Word, other believers, and circumstances to show us what he wants us to do. Praying for wisdom does not then mean sitting and waiting for revelation from heaven. It means asking, seeking, and knocking on every door God has available.

Jesus promised that those who put their faith in him could never lose their salvation. John 10:27–28 says, "My sheep listen to my voice; I know them, and they follow me. I give them eternal life, and they shall never perish; no one will snatch them out of my hand." Thank God for this promise that your salvation is secure, no matter how you may feel on any given day.

God promises to complete the good work that he has begun in you. Philippians 1:6 says, "Being confident of this, that he who began a good work in you will carry it on to completion until the day of Christ Jesus." It may feel like your growth is slow—one step forward, two steps back—but God is at work, and God will finish what he has begun. Think about what you looked like, on the inside, before you began following Jesus. Compare that to what you see now. Those areas of growth are proof of God's faithfulness. It doesn't mean that you have achieved victory in every area of struggle, but change comes through the power of the Holy Spirit in your life.

God has promised to cleanse you of all your sins when you confess them. First John 1:9 says, "If we confess our sins, he is faithful and just and will forgive us our sins and purify us from all unrighteousness." God is faithful and righteous. Because of Christ's sacrifice, you have been made righteous too.

One promise God makes to all believers is the promise that he will never leave us or forsake us. Joshua 1:5 says, "No one will be able to stand against you all the days of your life. As I was with Moses, so I will be with you; I will never leave you nor forsake you."

When you are tempted to sin, God promises to provide a way out. First Corinthians 10:13 says, "No temptation has overtaken you except what is common to mankind. And God is faithful; he will not let you be tempted beyond what you can bear. But when you are tempted, he will also provide a way out so that you can endure it." Think about a time when you were tempted to sin. Maybe you were tempted to flirt with a married coworker. Or maybe you were tempted to lie to get yourself out of trouble. How did God show up for you in whatever situation you were in?

Today, remember the ways God has kept his promises. Reflect on what you know of God's character. And trust that he will be faithful in the future.

Release the Lies

Take a deep breath in and slowly release it. As you continue to breathe, slowly and deeply, practice proclaiming your trust in God.

Inhale: "God, your words are true."

Exhale: "I trust you."

Inhale: "Your words are true."

Exhale: "I trust you."

Consider this your invitation to slow down and center your heart on the truth of God's character and his love for you. God is good. His love and mercy never end. And he has promised to be with you always.

Pause and take another deep breath, breathing in God's promises and breathing out doubt and fear. Each time doubt that God will keep his promises crops up in your mind, repeat the words, "Your words are true."

If you hear in your mind, "God has left you alone. You are not good enough for him," repeat the words from Joshua 1:5: "I will never leave you nor forsake you."

If you hear, "Your sins are too bad and too many; they can never be forgiven," repeat the words from 1 John 1:9: "If we confess our sins, he is faithful and just and will forgive us our sins and purify us from all unrighteousness."

Counter the lies you hear with the truth from God's Word. His promises are always true. To know what God says, you must be spending time in his Word, the Bible. Commit to studying Scripture so you can fight the lies of the enemy with this mighty sword of the Spirit.

Faithful God, I haven't done anything to deserve the great promises you've given me, but you are full of grace. Your mercy and kindness and faithfulness are never-ending. I trust you because you have been faithful to your people from generation to generation. Help me to trust you more every day. Thank you for your faithfulness to me. In the name of Jesus I pray, amen.

JOURNAL PROMPT: What are some promises of God you have clung to in the past? What are some promises you can apply to your life right now?

You Are Armed for Battle

Reflect on God's Word

Soldiers train in boot camp to develop strategies and strength to protect their country against enemies both foreign and domestic. They work tirelessly to be in shape so when they are called up, they are ready. They have strength and endurance to face their enemy. When they know an actual battle is coming, it's also important for them to know the strategy. Where are they going? Who are they fighting? What's the battle plan?

When you face a test of your faith, it might be easy to think you are not equipped to handle it. Maybe you haven't been following Jesus for very long, so you feel like you don't know enough to be able to withstand the schemes of the devil (Ephesians 6:11). Maybe you are just tired of fighting. Don't give up!

We live in a world and culture that opposes God's truth and the way of Christ, and Scripture provides a clear understanding about the real nature of our struggle with evil and the forces of darkness. Ephesians 6:12 tells us, "For our struggle is not against flesh and blood, but against the rulers, against the authorities, against the powers of this dark world and against the spiritual forces of evil in the heavenly realms."

Scripture also tells us that we have everything we need to fight these battles. Second Timothy 3:16–17 says, "All Scripture is God-breathed and is useful for teaching, rebuking, correcting and training in righteousness, so that the servant of God may be thoroughly equipped for every good work." Knowing Scripture so you can counter Satan's attacks is vital.

When Jesus was tempted by Satan in the wilderness, he countered every word of Satan's with God's Word. Matthew 4:1–11 (ESV) shows us:

> Then Jesus was led up by the Spirit into the wilderness to be tempted by the devil. And after fasting forty days and forty nights, he was hungry. And the tempter came and said to him, "If you are the Son of God, command these stones to become loaves of bread." But he answered, "It is written,
>
> > "'Man shall not live by bread alone,
> > > but by every word that comes from the
> > > mouth of God.'"
>
> Then the devil took him to the holy city and set him on the pinnacle of the temple and said to him, "If you are the Son of God, throw yourself down, for it is written,

    "'He will command his angels
        concerning you,'

and

    "'On their hands they will bear you up,
        lest you strike your foot against a stone.'"

Jesus said to him, "Again it is written, 'You shall not put the Lord your God to the test.'" Again, the devil took him to a very high mountain and showed him all the kingdoms of the world and their glory. And he said to him, "All these I will give you, if you will fall down and worship me." Then Jesus said to him, "Be gone, Satan! For it is written,

    "'You shall worship the Lord your God
        and him only shall you serve.'"

Then the devil left him, and behold, angels came and were ministering to him.

We are also given armor to help protect us and to help us fight. Ephesians 6:14–17 (ESV) says, "Stand therefore, having fastened on the belt of truth, and having put on the breastplate of righteousness, and, as shoes for your feet, having put on the readiness given by the gospel of peace. In all circumstances take up the shield of faith, with which you can extinguish all the flaming darts of the evil one; and take the helmet of salvation, and the sword of the Spirit, which is the word of God."

Truth, righteousness, peace, faith, salvation, the word of God—these are tools at your disposal, ready to be used in your battle.

Release the Lies

For just a moment, relax and settle your mind. Now position yourself before God, knowing that you have been equipped and are prepared for spiritual battle. Remember, you do not head into battle alone. He is with you the whole time.

Slowly stretch your neck to the left and then to the right. Gently and slowly twist your body to the left and then to the right, taking in slow breaths. Open your mind and your hands to allow God to equip you with his Word.

Are you weary and ready to give up the fight? Do you think there's no way restoration can come? Release those lies and replace them with the truth of God's Word.

The moment you accept Jesus as your Savior, you are given access to everything that you need to fight evil. You are never left on your own. The provision is automatic; all you have to do is use it. So when you hear that you cannot possibly be loved because of all you've done in your past, you can tell the evil one, "God tells me, 'I have loved you with an everlasting love'" (Jeremiah 31:3 ESV).

When you hear, "You'll never get over that sin," tell

the evil one, "God tells me, 'As far as the east is from the west, so far does he remove our transgressions from us'" (Psalm 103:12 ESV).

Take a moment now to identify the lies that are causing you to live in fear and defeat. Maybe you tell yourself, *I may as well give up. My marriage isn't going to get any better* or *My child is never going to have a change of heart* or *This addiction is more than I can handle.*

What does the truth of God's Word tell you about those lies? The truth is that your spouse is not your enemy, your child is not your enemy, you own body is not your enemy. The battle rages in the spiritual realm.

So don't give up! God sees your pain. Name it before the Lord. Let him uphold you and carry you through the battle. Now take a moment to pray about those people or situations in your life that need God's help. Fight back with truth from God's Word. Your marriage is worth it, your child is in God's hands, you can overcome your addiction.

Take a moment to rest here with God. Tell him that you trust him to equip you. Embrace in full confidence that he stands ready to fight for you in the battles in your life.

Lord Jesus, give me strength for the battle and endurance to seek your will. I've never felt weaker or more defeated in the battle against evil. Graciously release within me your gifts of faith, hope, love, discernment, and praise. In your mercy, hold me upright in the strength of your might. May I lean into your

word as my protection. Increase my faith to overcome temptation. Cover me with your protection. In
the name of Jesus, bind every evil spirit trying to cap-
ture my heart and mind. I need your light to see, your
encouragement to persevere, and your grace to resist
the enemy and then watch him flee from me. Equip
me with truth. In the mighty name of Jesus, amen.

JOURNAL PROMPT: In what areas of your life do you
feel battle-weary? Take a moment to write them down. Now
write out your own prayer, asking God to help you keep your
eyes on him and hang on to the strong name of Jesus.

Stilled by the Voice of Jesus

Reflect on God's Word

In Matthew 14:28–31 we read a brief but significant story about Peter doing something he probably had never imagined doing. He and Jesus' other disciples found themselves on a boat in the middle of the night when a storm came up. As the waves battered them, they saw something they couldn't believe: Jesus, walking toward them on the water! Peter said, "Lord, if it's you, tell me to come to you on the water."

Then Jesus spoke just one word to Peter: "Come." Matthew tells us, "Then Peter got down out of the boat, walked on the water and came toward Jesus. But when he saw the wind, he was afraid and, beginning to sink, cried out, 'Lord, save me!' Immediately Jesus reached out his hand and caught him. 'You of little faith,' he said, 'why did you doubt?'" (Matthew 14:28–31).

All Jesus' disciples remained on the boat; Peter was the only one to step onto the water. Perhaps if some of his friends had joined him, he wouldn't have felt as afraid. Picture the scene. Do you see yourself on the boat—watching from the side—or on the water?

Have you ever been invited to do something new, something you never thought of doing? What thoughts went through your mind? Were you just excited, or did you start to hear a voice in your head telling you everything that could go wrong?

Did that voice say, *People might not like you; you might not be any good at it; you might get lost, or hurt, or . . .?*

Now imagine you are Peter, being invited by Jesus to do something crazy, something he never thought he'd ever do. Feel the boat rocking in the pitch-black storm and the spray of water hitting your face. Watch as Jesus comes toward you, walking on the water. Suddenly you can't wait. What compels you to move toward him?

Is it that you believe that Jesus can enable you to walk on water? Did you forget to think about the wind? Feel it now coming at you—wild, harsh, whipping you off your feet—an unexpected threat. You were confident you wouldn't sink, but now you wonder if you'll be blown away.

Then Jesus grabs you, and you feel yourself steady. You realize that Jesus is powerful enough to save you from both the expected and the unexpected threats.

Jesus may not be calling you to walk on water, but he is certainly calling you to fix your eyes on him. As your faith wavers, as fear fills your heart, as your mind fills with doubts, fix your eyes on Jesus. When you're focused on Jesus, everything that's not essential slips away. And all that's left is all that really matters: Jesus.

Release the Lies

Maybe you've been listening to lies for a long time. They can sound like the voice of a parent telling you you'll never amount to anything. They can sound like a friend telling you that the behaviors you engaged in before you knew Jesus are still okay. Maybe they sound like your past, bringing up stuff already confessed. Listening only to the voice of Jesus, keeping your eyes only on him, will take some time. So sit up a little straighter now, and take a few deep breaths. Calm your mind and your heart.

Ask God to help change your first impulses. It's like muscle memory. When you've been used to hearing something for so long, your automatic response kicks in. Forging new pathways in your brain and training your heart to hear truth will give you the victory that you want over the lies you have believed.

Ask God to help you always listen to Jesus first. As you take another deep breath, feel your body rooting downward, your feet steady beneath you, your legs strong. In this secure stance, feel your head lifting toward the sky and your shoulders dropping. You stand firm here because your focus is on Jesus, who makes you stand firm. Breathe and feel that security in your body.

Close your eyes and listen for the voice of Jesus. His will be the gentle, small voice, the voice of love. He will never berate or condemn. He will never bring up the past, and he will always give you hope for your future.

If doubts start to fill your mind today, remind yourself to listen only to the voice of Jesus.

Heavenly Father, I've listened to lies for so long. Every day, they cause my mind to falter. My heart fails. My will grows weak. Help me to listen only to you, Lord, and to find in you everything I need to walk by faith and to shut down the lies. Thank you for sending your Son, Jesus, to teach me how to listen only to his voice. Thank you for calling me to follow you. In his name I pray, amen.

JOURNAL PROMPT: What truth is Jesus saying to you in the midst of your cares? One word? Two words? A question or challenge? What does his voice sound like to you?

Our Weakness, His Strength

Reflect on God's Word

During the 1992 Summer Olympic Games in Barcelona, Spain, British sprinter Derek Redmond tore his hamstring while running the 400-meter race. Seized with great pain, Redmond knew his race was over, but he still wanted to make it to the finish line. He kept on, hobbling painfully. And then suddenly, out of the stands, a man came running, brushing aside security, to support the limping athlete, his son. The two crossed the finish line together. What an iconic Olympic moment.[1]

And what a powerful visual image of a father helping his child. Hold that image in your head for a moment and imagine your heavenly Father supporting you when you feel weak and powerless, struggling to reach a finish line.

The enemy may tempt you to look for strength in the wrong places—in personal victories, a swelling bank account, a full cup of coffee—but the truth is that real strength comes from God. The prophet Isaiah promises, "Those who hope in the LORD will renew their strength. They will soar on wings like eagles; they will run and not grow weary, they will walk and not be faint" (Isaiah 40:31). When you call out to

God, God will come to your rescue and give you everything you need to soar with eagles.

We see this truth over and over again in Scripture.

Job is a prime example of relying on God's strength. He had just learned that all his children and servants had been killed, and all his livestock had been stolen. His words in Job 1:21–22 show his reliance on the Lord: "'Naked I came from my mother's womb, and naked I will depart. The LORD gave and the LORD has taken away; may the name of the LORD be praised.' In all this, Job did not sin by charging God with wrongdoing."

Job never could have endured all that happened to him without the strength of God upholding him.

Daniel, who was a faithful Hebrew, exiled in Babylon as a slave, faced many situations where he was in danger from the wrath of King Nebuchadnezzar. When he refused to stop praying to the one true God, he was thrown into a den of hungry lions. Darius, who had come to value Daniel as a wise advisor, reacts this way:

> When he came near the den, he called to Daniel in an anguished voice, "Daniel, servant of the living God, has your God, whom you serve continually, been able to rescue you from the lions?"
>
> Daniel answered, "May the king live forever! My God sent his angel, and he shut the mouths of the lions. They have not hurt me, because I was found innocent in his sight. Nor have I ever done any wrong before you, Your Majesty."

The king was overjoyed and gave orders to lift Daniel out of the den. And when Daniel was lifted from the den, no wound was found on him, because he had trusted in his God. (Daniel 6:20–23)

Without God's help—shutting the mouths of the lions—Daniel would surely have perished.

The apostle Paul endured many trials as he spread the gospel to the nations. Second Corinthians 11:24–30 (NLT) lists them:

Five different times the Jewish leaders gave me thirty-nine lashes. Three times I was beaten with rods. Once I was stoned. Three times I was shipwrecked. Once I spent a whole night and a day adrift at sea. I have traveled on many long journeys. I have faced danger from rivers and from robbers. I have faced danger from my own people, the Jews, as well as from the Gentiles. I have faced danger in the cities, in the deserts, and on the seas. And I have faced danger from men who claim to be believers but are not. I have worked hard and long, enduring many sleepless nights. I have been hungry and thirsty and have often gone without food. I have shivered in the cold, without enough clothing to keep me warm.

Then, besides all this, I have the daily burden of my concern for all the churches. Who is weak without my feeling that weakness? Who is led astray, and I do not burn with anger?

If I must boast, I would rather boast about the things that show how weak I am.

Weakness is not a failing. In fact, being aware of your weakness is the beginning of developing your strength because the strength God gives is strength *for his purposes*, for the race he has set out for you. This strength lifts you closer to him and enables you to do what he calls you to do.

Release the Lies

Take a deep breath and exhale slowly. Where do you feel weak? Give this question space to expand within you.

As you return to your breath, begin to notice it moving in and out, this simple, natural movement bringing life and health to your body. As you breathe, do a quick inventory of your body. Do you have weakness anywhere? In your back? Shoulders? Knees? Then think about the places you feel weak in life—marriage, parenting, work. Ask God to strengthen you.

Now think about places in your body you feel strong. Your arms? Your legs? And what about life? Maybe you feel strong in life because you've got the education, the training, the knowledge, the energy to carry out your job. If you're a teacher, you know how to teach. If you're a nurse, you know how to take care of people.

Take some time now to sit with another question: Where do you see yourself depending on your own strength rather than relying on God's strength?

When Satan tries to discourage you, go back to what you know is true: God gives strength to the weary and increases the power of the weak (Isaiah 40:29). He who began a good work in you will carry it on to completion (Philippians 1:6). Christ's power is made perfect in weakness (2 Corinthians 12:9).

Ask God to deliver you from Satan's lie that you have to do everything in your own power. Ask him to give you strength to soar like the eagles.

> God, I wait on you. Help me to understand both my weaknesses and my strengths. I believe that in my weakness, you are strong and will fight on my behalf. Help me to thank you for my strengths but not depend solely on them. Remind me that only you can deliver me and give me all I need. Thank you for sending Jesus to take on flesh and sympathize with all my weaknesses. Thank you for saving me through him. It's in his name that I pray, amen.

JOURNAL PROMPT: Describe a time when your weakness challenged you to lean on God. Maybe you faced a challenge at work or a problem that you were tasked to solve, and you didn't even know where to start. Or maybe you needed to have a hard conversation with a friend and were afraid of what it would do to your friendship. How did God bring you victory?

You Are Not Meant to
Live Life Alone

Reflect on God's Word

Singer-songwriter Paul Simon wrote, "I am an island." Our culture definitely values independence, the "self-made" man or woman. Ever hear a toddler say, "I do it myself!"?

You may believe that you don't need other people, that you and God can handle whatever comes along. But God has a different, better way. During creation, as God declared everything he made "good," only one thing was "not good": that the one human he had made would be alone. So God created a helper for the first man, Adam. He brought forth someone who was like the man, but different in significant ways. Someone to help him work the garden. Someone he could share life with.

God made us for community, to share life with others, both the suffering and the joy ("Rejoice with those who rejoice; mourn with those who mourn," Romans 12:15). This is the point the apostle Paul was making in his letter to the church of Corinth when he wrote: "If one part suffers, every part suffers with it; if one part is honored, every part rejoices with it. Now you are the body of Christ, and each one of you is a part of it" (1 Corinthians 12:26–27).

Galatians 6:2 encourages us to "carry each other's burdens, and in this way you will fulfill the law of Christ." And Psalm 133:1 says, "How good and pleasant it is when God's people live together in unity!"

It's hard to let people into our own suffering, to admit that we can't handle the pain alone. It's easier to let them into our rejoicing, to celebrate success. But both are necessary and balance each other. Our success is only by the grace of God, and only the grace of God can heal our suffering.

Think of your own body. It is one. You have fingers and toes, eyes and ears, heart and lungs. Each organ, each part of your body is unique. Think of a time when you had a headache or an injury. Remember how the rest of your body stepped up to help take care of the weak or injured part?

Living life alone can be a huge burden to carry. You might not even realize that this mindset is a lie you have been believing. But think of all the times the world has worked to make you believe that you can do life by yourself.

The movie *Cast Away*, starring Tom Hanks, is about a FedEx executive, Chuck Noland, who survives a plane crash on his way to Malaysia. He survives on an inflatable life raft but finds himself on a completely deserted island. Washed ashore with him are several FedEx packages containing random things ordered by ordinary people. With perseverance and ingenuity, Chuck survives for four years on that island and eventually is rescued and returned to civilization.[2]

What is striking about this movie is that, while Chuck is alone and able to survive by his wits and the useful things he finds in the FedEx packages, he still feels isolated. In fact, he overcomes that to some extent by drawing a face on a volleyball. Chuck names the volleyball "Wilson" and spends the rest of his time on the island conversing with "Wilson" as if he were a person there with him.

Chuck felt his isolation and his need for community. He was able to survive, but how much better would it have been if there had been others around him to encourage and help? Survival stories are very popular, but God wants more for us than mere survival: He wants us to thrive.

Take a few moments to reflect on how God created you, in all your uniqueness, to be around others—those you work with or live with—and how he desires for you to share life with them. Remember today that God has not left you alone in this world, to do life by yourself, but has instead provided a community of people with whom to share your life.

Release the Lies

Relax for a few moments. Feel your toes. Wiggle them and then relax them. Feel your ankles. Relax them. Feel your legs and then let them go limp. Also let your hands and arms go limp.

Breathe in and exhale slowly. Feel the air leave your lungs. Breathe in again and think about the oxygen going into your blood, through your heart. Your whole body, each individual part, works together.

Take a deep breath and think about the things that are weighing you down. What burdens do you carry today?

Think about your relationship with God. How does he share your suffering? Feel yourself taking burdens off your shoulders one by one and placing them in the hands of Jesus. Feel his strength as he receives them. Look into his face and see him smile as he senses you trust him.

Now reflect on the people God has put in your life. How could they help you lift your burdens? How could you help them carry their suffering?

Take another deep breath. What can you rejoice about today? How has God honored you with a blessing? With whom could you share it today?

Calm your heart and take time now to remember moments of joy that recently made you smile. Remember the small acts of kindness others offered you, and remember the small acts of kindness you offered others.

Reflect on how you are not alone. God has placed others in your life. Imagine crawling into his lap, sharing your day, and hearing him say your name along with the names of others he has placed in your life.

Feel the joy of his embrace and the love of those he has placed around you.

Lord Jesus, sometimes I feel alone. Open my eyes to see the people you have put in my life. Thank you that I am not created to be alone in my suffering or rejoicing. Thank you for creating others to be with me, to shoulder the load as well as to rejoice with me. And thank you, Lord, that you are always with me, and your presence gives me peace. Fill me with your Holy Spirit, empowering me to live life with others. And fill me with strength and a compassionate heart. In your precious name, amen.

JOURNAL PROMPT: Do you feel God nudging you to share life with someone? Describe that nudge. How will you respond?

PART 3

FEAR

Finding Courage

Reflect on God's Word

How can you command someone to be strong and courageous? We usually think of courage as a feeling, and feelings are notoriously hard to control.

But in Joshua 1:9, God commands Joshua to be strong and courageous: "Have I not commanded you? Be strong and courageous. Do not be afraid; do not be discouraged, for the LORD your God will be with you wherever you go."

Before he died, Moses laid his hands on Joshua, and he "was filled with the spirit of wisdom" (Deuteronomy 34:9). The Israelites recognized him as their new leader, the one who would take them into the promised land. What a daunting task! After all, Moses left some big shoes to fill. "For no one has ever shown the mighty power or performed the awesome deeds that Moses did in the sight of all Israel" (Deuteronomy 34:12). And now the children of Israel are gathered around Joshua, awaiting his direction about what they are to do next.

The verses immediately preceding and following Joshua 1:9 encourage the Israelites that God is with them and will give them victory in battle. Three times God tells Joshua to be strong and courageous (vv. 6, 7, and 9). Was it because Joshua was wondering whether he was up to the task? Nowhere does God tell him to ignore fear or to pretend that the challenge before him isn't all that great. Instead, he assures Joshua—and the children of Israel—of his constant presence and that they will be victorious in battle.

We probably all have different ideas about what strength and courage look like. For some of us, strength refers to physical might. Other people might think of emotional resilience. Joshua was certainly facing physical hardship, but he was also about to leave the life he'd known for a very long time. Having courage for him meant trusting God with his physical and mental well-being; being strong meant carrying out God's commands. It meant believing that God meant it when he said, "I will never leave you nor forsake you" (v. 5). Joshua found courage in this promise. You can too.

Like Joshua, you can rely on the presence of God whenever you're feeling afraid. Whenever you come up against something too big to handle, remind yourself that God is with you and has promised to lead you. Instead of just hoping you feel brave enough for the circumstance, rejoice in his constant presence and never-failing guidance.

Like Joshua, you can choose to rejoice in the presence of God, no matter what is in front of you. And you can find courage.

Release Your Fear

Begin to analyze what you're afraid of. Perhaps you fear confronting someone about a way in which they hurt you, or something they're doing wrong. Maybe you have felt God calling you to right an injustice in your community. Or maybe you're moving to a new city, taking a new job, or starting college. All these can be fear-inducing circumstances. Acknowledge them, and then begin to embrace a posture of humility, admitting you're afraid and need help, so that you can receive strength and courage. Relax your body as much as you can and slow your breathing. Find a good rhythm and a comfortable position that will allow you to turn your thoughts inward.

Reflect on a time in your past that required courage. Spend a moment dissecting your process. Try to remember details of the way God helped you. Perhaps he sent along a friend or a kind word at just the right time. Maybe he used Scripture to help you be courageous. How did you see God work on your behalf?

Now, spend a moment thinking about the things going on in your life right now. Focus on anything causing you anxiety. Now focus on the fact that God will give you the strength to deal with it. He is saying to you just as he said to Joshua, "Only be strong and courageous" (Joshua 1:18). Ask a friend to pray for you as you determine to take the step God is asking you to take.

You don't have to wait until you *feel* brave to be strong and courageous. You have the support of the God who controls the wind and the waves, and he promises to be with you. Look for ways to lean on that support today in your job, in your home, in your relationships. Focus on God instead of the storms around you, and he will get you through whatever it is that's in your way.

> Lord, thank you so much for your attention to my life. I am humbled by the fact that you care for me. Help me remember that your presence is enough to help me become strong and courageous when I am confronted with something that threatens to create fear in my life. I know you are the source of my strength and courage, and I'm so grateful you would provide that for me! Open my heart today to rejoice in your goodness and my mind to understand your truth. In your Son's holy name I pray, amen.

JOURNAL PROMPT: Write about some challenging situations you face at work, at home, or in relationships. How might seeking God's presence in these situations help you find courage to face them?

Courage under Fire

Reflect on God's Word

Have you ever faced a life-or-death situation because of your faith? Or done something that caused you to be unfaithful to God?

Jewish exiles Shadrach, Meshach, and Abednego had to choose between obeying God or obeying a direct order from the Babylonian king ruling over them. The king had issued a decree that everyone must bow down to a golden idol, proclaiming that anyone who did not do so would be thrown into a fiery furnace.

Daniel 3:16–18 describes how Shadrach, Meshach, and Abednego responded to the king's decree: "King Nebuchadnezzar, we do not need to defend ourselves before you in this matter. If we are thrown into the blazing furnace, the God we serve is able to deliver us from it, and he will deliver us from Your Majesty's hand. But even if he does not, we want you to know, Your Majesty, that we will not serve your gods or worship the image of gold you have set up."

Imagine being one of these three Jewish men.

Perhaps, as you make your courageous statement to the king, you hope God will save you by softening the king's heart.

But as you finish speaking, you see the look on the king's face. He is furious! Suddenly, you find yourself sweating.

The king then flies into a rage, commanding his men to make the fire seven times hotter than usual. He also demands they tie you up. Your skin begins to sting and burn, and the rough ropes chafe against your skin.

And then you find yourself surrounded by fire, a fire so hot that it incinerates the soldier who throws you into it. Your ropes burn off, but much to your surprise, nothing else burns! In fact, you discover you can walk freely through the flames. As you struggle to make sense of it, you realize you're not alone in the fire. Another person stands near you: the Lord. He is with you in the fire. Deep peace fills your heart.

The stunned king calls you to come out of the fire, and you walk out, unharmed, not even smelling of smoke. The king begins praising God, proclaiming that no one can ever speak ill of the true God.

You realize that your courageous faith has brought glory to God in a way you never could have imagined.

Today, let God's love for you and his mighty strength be the solid ground you stand on—your sure and certain truth, the embrace that holds you when you're afraid. Remember that God doesn't promise you will escape persecution for your faith, but he *does* promise to be with you in the flames.

Release Your Fear

Perhaps your heart is already beating faster at the prospect of following God into something that might put your security or safety at risk. Take a deep breath. God is with you. Let his strength fill you. Feel it lifting your head as your shoulders sink down. Feel yourself growing taller, more relaxed, and more centered as you continue inhaling deeply and exhaling deeply, remembering that God is your strength.

Shadrach, Meshach, and Abednego understood God's power and believed that he was mighty enough to save them from the king's wrath and from the blazing furnace. Do you believe that God has the power to deliver you from whatever fiery trials you face?

These men had faith in God's power, and yet they did not presume to know God's will. They accepted that God's plan might be different from their desires.

Take another deep breath and consider the risk those three men took in order to stay faithful to God. Then, as you exhale, consider your own situation and the risk you may need to take in order to stay faithful to God.

Breathe in again deeply and exhale, handing your situation to God and reaffirming your trust in him, whatever the outcome.

Heavenly Father, please fill me with the kind of courageous faith that Shadrach, Meshach, and Abednego had. Help me to trust you despite my circumstances. Thank you for promising to be with me in every trial. All the power and the glory in heaven and on earth are yours, God—may my life testify to that truth even in fiery trials. In the name of Jesus I pray, amen.

JOURNAL PROMPT: How has God called you in the past to stand courageously in your faith for him? What happened to you and to those around you?

Trusting Your Child to God

Reflect on God's Word

One of the greatest desires of parents who follow Jesus is that their kids would follow Jesus too.

Trouble is, as we all know, that doesn't always happen, no matter how many Sunday school classes, family devotionals, and prayer times you guide them through as they grow up. It's heartbreaking to watch.

There are different levels of rebellion that parents face. Some are still able to have meaningful, loving relationships with their kids who have walked away from the Lord, while others battle the heartbreak of addiction, lawlessness, and a complete break from the family. Whatever your circumstance, you and your child are never out of the heavenly Father's care.

God's kindness is meant to lead your wayward child to repentance. His kindness is meant to show us that he has always loved us. Romans 2:4 says, "Or do you show contempt for the riches of his kindness, forbearance and patience, not realizing that God's kindness is intended to lead you to repentance?" As you consider this verse, let God speak to your heart about your relationship with him, and with your child.

There may be times in your journey with your child when you feel taken advantage of, when you feel that they are presuming upon your kindness, forbearance, and patience. As you consider your own relationship with God, what parallels do you see with your child's relationship with you?

Have you ever decided to do something you know breaks the heart of God because you knew you would be forgiven for it? That God would never turn away from you? It's his very loving character that gives you the freedom to believe that, no matter how misguided that idea may be. As a parent, you know there is nothing your child could do that would cause you to stop loving them, but you fear for how their behavior is going to affect their life.

If you have a child who has fallen into addiction and other destructive behaviors, it may feel like you're constantly waiting for the other shoe to drop. Will you get a call from the police, or the hospital? You can't sleep wondering what's happening to your child. Maybe it feels like peace will never come.

Please know that you are not alone. God is still good. He still loves you and your child. Take a few moments to feel God's arms surround you. Acknowledge those feelings, and then take a deep breath and feel the presence of God in your turmoil.

As you've acknowledged your feelings of uncertainty and chaos, the challenge is for you to change your mindset. You might find yourself constantly asking, "What if?" *What if my child gets arrested? What if they fall in with the wrong crowd? What if they overdose? What if they never turn to Jesus?*

Let yourself ask those questions.

And then do this: Instead of asking "What if?" say "Even if." Even if the absolute worst-case scenario happens, does that change the goodness of God? Your perception of who God is will make a huge difference in how you relate to your child. If you believe God is who he says he is, and he can do what he says he can do, then you can be at peace. It doesn't mean that you won't be heartbroken over the decisions your child makes, but you can know that ultimately God is still good.

So what does this change of mind look like? Author Katherine James describes when her son overdosed on heroin and was fighting for his life in the hospital. In the elevator on the way to the critical care unit, she says,

> I watched as the numbers above the doors slowly climbed and reminded myself of the most basic of Christian tenets: trust God—and it's not a platitude if you say it to yourself. But I couldn't trust him because our son could die. But there was no other option. I thought about what it would be like if Sweetboy died; but then, as though the Holy-Spirit-Bird had just landed on my shoulder, I understood that it would be okay no matter what. However fleeting, at least for that one moment in the elevator, I felt a complete peace.[1]

Even if your child should die of a drug overdose. Even if your daughter were to get pregnant out of wedlock. Even if your son should end up in prison. None of that changes the goodness of God, nor does it change your standing in his eyes. He loves you so much.

And God's kindness is meant to lead our children—and us—to repentance. Your love and kindness to your child is an extension of that. Great wisdom is needed to know what that kindness and love look like.

There's always talk about tough love. Maybe you need to tell your child they can no longer live in your house. Maybe it means not bailing them out financially if their foolish choices lead them to difficulty paying rent. But maybe grace is what is needed more. Maybe you purchase a housewarming gift even though they've moved in with their boyfriend or girlfriend. Perhaps it looks like helping to care for that grandchild who might have to be given up for adoption if the young, unmarried couple doesn't get practical help.

These decisions can be agonizing for a parent who simply loves their child until they think their heart will burst inside their chest. When you see your worst fear for your child happening, you may be tempted to give up hope, to cease to believe that God cares.

Maybe it's strange to talk about poker in a Christian devotion, but there's a saying among poker players: a chip and a chair. As long as you've still got one chip and a chair at the table, you're not out of the game. As long as your child still has breath in their body, God's Spirit can woo them back to him.

God's got this. Trust Him. Walk with him. Abide in him.

And even if your child never does come back to the Lord, your eternal relationship with God is still secure.

Release Your Fear

Breathe deeply and slowly, letting your mind and your heart be calm before the Lord. Picture yourself sitting face-to-face with your heavenly Father and holding his hands. God's kindness, not rules and regulations and persuasive speech, is what leads to repentance. Breathe in the loving-kindness of God as you sit in this time alone with him.

Consider this: God is the perfect parent, but his children still rebel and turn away from him. Ask him now to comfort you with his overwhelming love and to remind you of his great care for your kids.

When we interact with our wayward children, it's best to come with an attitude of humility—not thinking that we have our act together but that we are as much in need of grace and forgiveness as they are. Empty your heart now of anything that is hindering your fullhearted relationship with God. Pour it out to your heavenly Father. Ask God to give you great wisdom.

Now name what it is you fear about each child. Do you fear they will never walk with Jesus? That they will get into some addiction, be it alcohol, drugs, or pornography? Do you fear pregnancy from an unwed child? Place all these fears on the table before the Lord.

Now try that exercise mentioned earlier: For each fear, ask the Lord, "What if (fill in the blank) happens to my child?" Listen for his answer. What do you hear him say to you? Do this for each fear and see how the Lord brings you his peace. Because even if the worst-case scenario happens, God is still good.

> Father God, you know the pain of a wayward child. Your people rebelled against you in the past, and your beloved children rebel against you still today. Show me how to love and not to fear. Help me not to grow weary in doing good, but to depend on your Holy Spirit for the strength and the wisdom I need. Help me to make the right choices for myself, my family, and my child. I know it's not going to be easy. I want more than anything for my child to walk with you. But I know that you want that even more than I do. Help me to trust you for the wisdom I need and for the strength to love my child as you love them. Whether it be tough love or acts of kindness that show them how gracious you are, let me be doing what you want me to do. It's in the great name of Jesus that I pray, amen.

JOURNAL PROMPT: Write down those "What if?" statements from before. Now turn them into "Even if" statements and feel the difference that makes.

Safe with God

Reflect on God's Word

If you've lived in tornado country, you may be familiar with a storm cellar. You know that when a funnel cloud has been spotted, you grab your family and your pets and head to safety underground. Overhead, if the storm passes your way, you can hear the tumult, but you know you are safe.

In Psalm 119:114, David isn't talking about tornados, but his storm is just as real when he says to God, "You are my refuge and my shield; I have put my hope in your word."

Our God is strength. He is a safe place. A fortress. A solid rock. A storm cellar. No one else can be our refuge like him. He will protect us from the storms that threaten our peace and security and fill us with fear.

The psalms speak often of God as our refuge.

Psalm 32:7 says, "You are my hiding place; you will protect me from trouble and surround me with songs of deliverance."

Psalm 91:1–2 says, "Whoever dwells in the shelter of the Most High will rest in the shadow of the Almighty. I will say of the LORD, 'He is my refuge and my fortress, my God, in whom I trust.'"

Moses, thought to be the author of Psalm 91, spoke these words to the Israelites before his death as part of a larger song reminding God's people of all he had done for them:

> In a desert land he found him,
>> in a barren and howling waste.
> He shielded him and cared for him;
>> he guarded him as the apple of his eye,
> like an eagle that stirs up its nest
>> and hovers over its young,
> that spreads its wings to catch them
>> and carries them aloft.
> The Lord alone led him;
>> no foreign god was with him.
>> (Deuteronomy 32:10–12)

Sometimes, finding refuge in God and going to him when we are afraid means remembering what he has done for us in the past. Some commentators believe that King David's Psalm 32 was written after Psalm 51, in which he repents before God of his sin with Bathsheba (see 2 Samuel 11). In verses 1–6 of Psalm 32, David recounts how it felt to be forgiven by God. He counted himself blessed that God had forgiven his transgressions. And then verse 10 says, "Many are the woes of the wicked, but the Lord's unfailing love surrounds the one who trusts in him."

Picture a fortress being built. Every time you bring your fears before God, a new brick is placed on the structure. Your experience of security and peace grows with each prayer for protection, with each cry of your heart for God to surround you and be your security.

The thing about fortresses, storm cellars, and places of protection is that you have to actually *go to them* in order for them to help you. You can't simply know they're there. You have to flee to their shelter. When an attacking army was spotted entering an ancient kingdom or fief, the surrounding villages were evacuated to the fortress. Anyone who chose not to go would risk falling prey to the invaders. Unless they went *to* the fortress and hid themselves behind the strong walls, they were vulnerable.

What does fleeing to God when you are afraid look like? It's closeting yourself in prayer, immersing yourself in his Word. Pulling his salvation around your shoulders like a mantle. Reminding yourself of all that he has done for you in the past. In Psalm 56:3–4, David writes, "When I am afraid, I put my trust in you. In God, whose word I praise—in God I trust and am not afraid. What can mere mortals do to me?"

David often had occasion to be afraid. David Guzik, author of the popular online biblical commentary Enduring Word, says, "The young man who killed the lion and the bear, who killed Goliath, and was a successful young captain in Israel's army, did not deny the presence of fear. There were times when he was afraid. Yet he knew what to do with that fear, to boldly proclaim His trust in God despite the fear."[2]

Release Your Fear

Try to get a concrete picture in your mind of God as a refuge or shield. Imagine God as a literal hiding place, a place you go for rest from the battle or protection from your enemies. A refuge is where you run when you are in danger. A storm cellar.

God created refuge cities in ancient Israel so people who were wrongly accused or in danger could hide out in those cities. There they would be safe, cared for, and protected from harm.

Take a moment to close your eyes and take a deep breath, then imagine being in that safe place, a refuge city. What do you see? What do you hear? How do you feel? Does your heartbeat seem to slow?

Ask God now to rejuvenate you, to give you what you need to face the day with courage and joy, regardless of what comes.

As you begin to come out of the stillness of prayer, grab onto the things God spoke to you. Internalize them, ask him to help you remember that he is a safe place. He is the true hope, the true refuge, the true rest.

Oh, Refuge and Shield, you are my safe place. You are my rest. I can trust you because I know you are absolutely sovereign and perfectly good. Let me hide myself in you now. Don't let my heart be fooled into thinking that anyone or anything else can comfort, fulfill, or shelter me. Only you can. Remind me to run to you as my true hope, shelter, refuge, and God. Remind me that you care for me as a father cares for his child. You love me with an everlasting love. Teach my heart to trust you today. Build my faith, dear God. In Jesus' name, amen.

JOURNAL PROMPT: In what ways do you need God to be your refuge and shield today? What is one way you can choose to rest in him?

Trusting God through
Health Concerns

Reflect on God's Word

There is little that is as unsettling as a hospital. Unless you're in the labor and maternity ward welcoming new life, a hospital can be a very scary place. The stinging smell of hand sanitizer, the squeaky plastic chair bed, the constant beep, beep, beep of pulse-ox monitors up and down the hallway. When you or a loved one has extended stays in a hospital room, it all becomes so familiar that you can almost stop registering the details. It becomes just white noise.

While we may know intellectually that the hospital is a place of repair and healing, it can also be frightening and unsettling.

Spending any length of time at the hospital is draining—more than anything, it is the waiting that can pull out the obsessive in us. We madly scour old college textbooks, online medical journals, and Google for information that might predict the future like a crystal ball.

But nothing can tell us what happens next.

So we sit there holding our loved one's hand. We pour ourselves out until every last drop of us is gone, and then worry starts to seep in, filling every crevice of our tired, empty body.

But as worry fills us up, it leaves us dry and thirsty.

So, go before your Father God. Drop by drop, spill your worry at his feet.

He cares, so he listens. And gracefully, mercifully, he fills us up and over with peace.

It is peace that seems to be the opposite of what you feel in such a place—the sort of peace that strengthens your heart as you look to tomorrow and shields your mind against anxious, fearful thoughts.

Again and again, every day, go to God. Tell him your worries and ask for his peace. And this you can know about your God: He is faithful.

The lie worry tells you is this: God doesn't care.

But here's the truth as it is written in Psalm 118:1, 5–6 (CSB):

> Give thanks to the LORD, for he is good;
> his faithful love endures forever. . . .
> I called to the LORD in distress;
> the LORD answered me
> and put me in a spacious place.
> The LORD is for me; I will not be afraid.

He is good, he hears our cries, he is for us. We need not be afraid.

Do you feel the pain and relief and dullness of this place

acutely? Maybe you know what it is to hand your screaming baby over to doctors with hope and fear tangled together in your heart. You know what it is to hear "yes, but" and "no, unless."

Maybe you know what it means to want your loved one healed so badly that your insides pulse with a constant, throbbing pain.

Jesus encountered a man named Jairus one day. He was a synagogue leader and had a young daughter who was very sick, even dying. Mark 5:23 tells us Jairus "pleaded earnestly with him, 'My little daughter is dying. Please come and put your hands on her so that she will be healed and live.'"

And so Jesus went with him, stopping along the way to heal a woman who had an issue of blood for twelve years. But after that pause, people from Jairus's household came and told him his daughter had died, that he shouldn't bother Jesus anymore. Can you imagine how Jairus felt at that moment? He had come to Jesus because he knew that Jesus could heal his daughter. And then the bottom dropped out of his stomach as he heard this news.

But Jesus went anyway, knowing what he would do, knowing that this miracle of bringing Jairus's daughter back to life would bring God more glory.

But you don't know the outcome of your prayers, do you? And you feel afraid. But still, like Jairus, you get on your knees and beg Jesus. There is no dignity in your begging; you crouch next to the hospital bed and, like Jairus, plead for healing.

But even as you ask the Great Physician for a miracle, remember this: whether the answer is yes or no, he is good.

God's character does not change. If he was good yesterday in health, he is good today in sickness. He can be nothing but goodness, grace, and light. We also know that he is able. Cling to that knowledge as you pray.

Psalm 54:4 (CSB) says, "God is my helper; the Lord is the sustainer of my life." So we turn to Jesus because he knows the depth of our longing and will answer us. There is not one breath that we take that he does not give us. The fact is, our days are numbered.

Psalm 139:16 tells us, "Your eyes saw my unformed body; all the days ordained for me were written in your book before one of them came to be."

Release Your Fear

Imagine yourself in the throne room of the Lord. Kneel before him or bow your head in submission to him and know that he is both sovereign King and compassionate Father. As you picture yourself in the presence of God, know that he sees you and he loves you.

Now give God your anxiety. Unburden your heart and tell him your worries. As you think of your situation right now, admit to God that you are afraid he might say no. Now ask him for your wildest hope. As Jairus did, tell him your heart and ask him for a miracle.

Hear Jesus' words: "Don't be afraid; just believe" (Mark 5:36). Trust him to do all that is for your good and his glory.

Here's the hard part—the exercise in trust. Repeat what Jesus prayed in the Lord's Prayer and again in the garden of Gethsemane: "Your will be done."

Father God, this seems uncontrollable. But you are the one who knows tomorrow and knows next year. Take these worries from me and replace them with peace. Take my fear and give me trust. Let me know from the depths of my soul that you are for me and give me the strength to face whatever comes. I am brokenhearted as I come before you. I have nothing to give, but I want to trust you because I know you are trustworthy. You are Glory as you weave your sovereign plan; You are Grace as you listen to my plea. You are Power, and you can heal. So I ask that you would. But if you do not, Lord, help my heart. Allow me to trust you, to lean into you, as you are Peace. Your will be done. In Jesus' name, amen.

JOURNAL PROMPT: Write out the worries and anxieties you're giving to God. What is he saying in return?

PART 4

LONELINESS

Alone but Not Lonely

Reflect on God's Word

Is it hard for you to be alone? Do feelings of loneliness dominate your time by yourself? Being alone does not always mean feeling lonely. That's not to say that you need to deny your feelings of loneliness. God wants you to bring your cares to him. But when these feelings and thoughts take over your waking hours, you can feel constantly weighed down by them. It is true that when we spend a lot of time alone, we can more easily begin to feel unloved. And because we are created in the image of a triune God and are therefore made for community, when we spend a lot of time alone, loneliness can overtake us. But that doesn't have to be the case.

God invites us to trust him with our time and with our relationships. Jeremiah 29:11 is often quoted to reassure people going through a hard time: "'For I know the plans I have for you,' declares the Lord, 'plans to prosper you and not to harm you, plans to give you hope and a future.'" The next time you feel lonely, remind yourself of this verse. Cast your loneliness on him and trust that he knows your future, and that he has good plans for you. He wants you to trust him fully, even when you don't know what's ahead.

God encourages us to learn to spend time alone with him. He wants us to take time alone to care for ourselves by getting rest, participating in self-care activities like exercise, or learning about something that interests us. Times of being alone do not have to be boring and lonely. They can be soul-nurturing, body-invigorating, and mind-stimulating.

One of the ways we can nurture our souls is by turning our focus toward God. Do you regularly make time to spend with God? Books, podcasts, videos of sermons or talks, and Bible-reading plans are all resources that can help turn your eyes upon Jesus instead of your feelings of loneliness.

Self-care may look like getting more exercise, investing time in eating healthier, or reading a good book. What are some things that make you laugh? According to the Mayo Clinic, laughter can improve your immune system, relieve pain, increase personal satisfaction, and improve your mood.[1]

Stimulating your mind can take many forms. What subjects are you curious about? Is there a hobby like gardening or painting you can explore? Maybe you're good at sudoku or crossword puzzles. Not only can these activities keep your mind active, but according to Alzheimer's Society, brain training may also help stave off diseases like dementia.[2]

It's often true that the hardest and loneliest seasons in life are also the richest seasons. When all is dark, you become more attuned to moments of light. Whether you consider yourself an introvert or an extrovert, you can find refreshment from spending time alone.

Release Your Loneliness

Revel in this moment to invest in your relationship with God. This time is yours and the Lord's. Slow your breathing and rest your hands in your lap. Sit in a position that lets you feel relaxed. Sit with your feet flat on the floor and back straight, then take a few deep breaths.

Picture yourself sitting alone in a room full of people. What feelings come to your heart? Tell God about each one of them. Explore why you might be feeling those things. Feel the touch of God's hand of love on your head as you talk to him.

Now, listen to his words to you: "Come with me by yourselves to a quiet place and get some rest" (Mark 6:31).

The world is seemingly run by extroverts. Every commercial you see shows a large group of people having fun together, or even a small group of friends enjoying one another's company. It can give you the impression that being alone is bad. But in a harried world, being alone can be a gift.

The best thing you can do for your relationships, your work, and your own development is to cultivate a pattern of spending time alone with the Lord. During those moments he will renew you and guide you through the next steps of your life. You can trust in what he has planned for you. Make spending time alone with God a protected part of your daily routine.

And then consider how you can nurture your body and your mind. Is there a class you can sign up for? A podcast you can subscribe to? A cooking channel you can start watching?

Resist the temptation to think that because these things are not overtly spiritual that they are not worthwhile. Body, mind, and soul work together, just as Deuteronomy 6:5 instructs and Jesus reiterates in Matthew 22:37: "Love the LORD your God with all your heart and with all your soul and with all your mind."

> Gracious heavenly Father, I know I can trust you. Give me the courage to pursue you and take care of myself whenever feelings of loneliness weigh me down. Give me peace in spending time alone, with the knowledge that you are always there. Help me rest well, not in self-indulgence but in self-care that will renew me to pursue whatever future you have for me. Help me to trust you with my time today, to do things that will benefit my soul, my body, and my mind. Thank you for your guidance. In the holy name of Jesus I pray, amen.

JOURNAL PROMPT: What are some things you can do to nurture your relationship with God during times when you are alone? What are some activities you can do to take care of yourself?

Trusting God in Singleness

Reflect on God's Word

Every Hallmark movie ever made ends with either a wedding, or, at the very least, a proposal. Shows like *The Bachelor* and *Married at First Sight* glamorize getting married. In a culture inundated with the noise of romance, it can be easy to get bogged down in the loneliness you feel about being single.

For many, the most painful part of singleness is loneliness—a feeling that's amplified the more you see others together. It can leave you feeling left out, unloved, isolated, or like there's something wrong with you. It can be soul wearying.

How do you process loneliness when being alone is your current reality?

King Solomon teaches on the beauty of community when he writes in Ecclesiastes 4:9–12,

> Two are better than one,
>> because they have a good return for their
>> labor:
> If either of them falls down,
>> one can help the other up.

> But pity anyone who falls
>> and has no one to help them up.
> Also, if two lie down together, they will
>> keep warm.
>> But how can one keep warm alone?
> Though one may be overpowered,
>> two can defend themselves.
> A cord of three strands is not quickly broken.

This passage paints a powerful picture. Singleness doesn't mean you escape community. Even without a spouse, you still need people. Instead of letting loneliness send you into a spiral of disappointment or sadness, let it be an opportunity for you to engage with God and community. Even though you may not be married, you weren't designed to be alone.

The pull to be married can be very strong. So what do you do with that desire if there doesn't seem to be hope for it on the horizon? How do you keep walking with Jesus if disappointment weighs you down?

Consider where you can engage with other people. Churches can be great places to live life with others. Yes, often there is an emphasis on couples and families, so you might need to work a little harder. But even becoming involved in family life can be beneficial. Consider offering to babysit or take kids to the park. Volunteer with the elderly or shut-ins.

Scripture also commands us to rejoice with those who rejoice (Romans 12:15). When friends around you are dating and getting married, rejoice with them. It may feel like you're putting on a facade, so talk to God about it. Ask him to give you a heart of love for those around you who are celebrating.

Even though singleness might be your current reality, you are not left alone. Allow the presence of God to meet you in your loneliness. Let his nearness sustain you and bring you courage. Trust that God has a good plan for you. Proverbs 3:5–6 assures us that if we trust him, he will show us the way: "Trust in the LORD with all your heart and lean not on your own understanding; in all your ways submit to him, and he will make your paths straight."

Release Your Loneliness

Let the distractions fade away and allow yourself to be fully present in this moment. Ask God to make you sensitive to his presence, even in your loneliness. Appreciate the silence that gives you a chance to encounter God.

Take a deep breath in through your nose, and slowly let it out through your mouth. As you continue to sit quietly in God's presence, let his nearness be a comforting reminder that you are not alone.

Acknowledge any disappointment or sadness you may feel from the loneliness of being single. Confess to God where you have distrusted his goodness or tried to take control of your situation by pursuing relationships that are not healthy just so you could have companionship. Thank God for his faithfulness to forgive and ask him to restore where you feel inadequate and alone.

Ask yourself these questions: How have you seen companionship and friendship help you to succeed? How can you be a companion to other single friends who might be prone to isolate?

Instead of sinking into loneliness, allow this to be an opportunity to pursue community with those around you.

Consider how you might engage in your feelings of loneliness today so they will lead you into communion with Christ. Remember that he is near to you, he cares for you, and he is available to you at any moment. Let your feelings of loneliness find comfort in him as you trust him to show you your community.

God, these feelings of loneliness can be overwhelming, and it's easy for me to isolate. Help me to use this season to grow deeper in my relationship with you and to build community with others. Give me courage when things seem hard. Show me how to truly love others so I can rejoice with them. I didn't want this season of singleness, and the loneliness I feel is painful, but I know you love me and that you have a good plan for me. I want to use this as an opportunity to depend on you. Help me to be strong and courageous. It's in the precious name of Jesus that I pray, amen.

JOURNAL PROMPT: What are some steps you can take to engage in community? Determine to follow through on one of them this week.

Always Surrounded by Love

Reflect on God's Word

Have you ever felt lonely even when you're not alone?

Sometimes, loneliness strikes hardest when you're surrounded by people, but you feel disconnected from them or invisible to them. You feel no one notices you or cares about you. No one gets you. Other times, hours or days spent alone can leave you feeling utterly forgotten by the outside world.

You call out but hear only an echo. You reach out your hand but don't find anyone to clasp hands with you. Your voice grows weak. Your hand stays empty.

Loneliness is painful, and it can make your soul restless as you long for deep relationships.

When you're feeling lonely, tell God how you feel and put your hope in him. Join the psalmist in asking God to "turn to me and be gracious to me, for I am lonely and afflicted" (Psalm 25:16).

Though you may feel alone, you are never alone. Though you may feel unknown, God knows every hair on your head and every hurt in your heart. Verses 20 and 21 of that same psalm say, "Guard my life and rescue me; do not let me be put to shame, for I take refuge in you. May integrity and uprightness protect me, because my hope, LORD, is in you."

Rest in the comfort of God's presence. God is with you now, surrounding you with his great love.

He will hear your prayer and answer you. Maybe not in the way you expect. Maybe not on the timetable you'd pre-fer. But put your trust in God, and he will lead you through loneliness with his steadfast love.

King David, who wrote Psalm 25, knew loneliness and affliction. He was often in great physical danger. But this psalm is rich in truth. Let David's words remind you of God's great love:

> I trust in you;
>> do not let me be put to shame,
>> nor let my enemies triumph over me.
> No one who hopes in you
>> will ever be put to shame,
> but shame will come on those
>> who are treacherous without cause. . . .
>
> Guide me in your truth and teach me,
>> for you are God my Savior,
>> and my hope is in you all day long.
> Remember, LORD, your great mercy and love,
>> for they are from of old. . . .

Good and upright is the LORD;
  therefore he instructs sinners in his ways.
He guides the humble in what is right
  and teaches them his way.
All the ways of the LORD are loving and
    faithful
  toward those who keep the demands of
    his covenant.
For the sake of your name, LORD,
  forgive my iniquity, though it is great.

My eyes are ever on the LORD,
  for only he will release my
    feet from the snare.
      (Psalm 25:2–3, 5–6, 8–11, 15)

Jesus understands the pain of loneliness like no one else does. Isaiah 53:2–5 describes the Messiah. Try to imagine Jesus as he's described here:

He grew up before him like a tender shoot,
  and like a root out of dry ground.
He had no beauty or majesty to attract us
    to him,
  nothing in his appearance that we should
    desire him.
He was despised and rejected by mankind,

> a man of suffering, and familiar
>> with pain.
> Like one from whom people hide their faces
>> he was despised, and we held him in low
>>> esteem.
>
> Surely he took up our pain
>> and bore our suffering,
> yet we considered him punished by God,
>> stricken by him, and afflicted.
> But he was pierced for our transgressions,
>> he was crushed for our iniquities;
> the punishment that brought us peace was
>> on him,
>> and by his wounds we are healed.

Jesus can sympathize with all your weaknesses, your sorrow, and your needs. By his wounds, you are healed. Ask Jesus to bring healing to your heart today.

This is the promise of God: that even in your loneliness, you are never alone. God's love always surrounds you.

Release Your Loneliness

One of the dangers of loneliness is that it can cause us to become more and more self-focused, caught up in our own sadness and isolation.

Are you open to what God has to give you today, to the ways God wants to provide for you in your loneliness? As you take a deep breath, hold out your hands, asking God to fill them. Touch your eyes, asking God to change your perspective, giving you eyes to see the people he's put in your life who might need you to be a friend to them.

Now think back to the loneliest times in your life. How did the Lord minister to you in those seasons? Perhaps there was a Scripture that spoke to you, or a person God sent to you. Take a moment and reflect on the ways God provided for you during lonely times in the past. How can you do the same for others?

Let your loneliness draw you nearer to the God of light and all comfort.

Jesus, you know what it feels like to be forsaken by all your closest friends. You were a man of sorrows; you were acquainted with grief. Please comfort me in my loneliness and help me give you thanks for this challenging season. Teach me how to trust you even in the darkest stretches. Stay with me and let me taste the sweetness of your presence. Thank you for taking on flesh and coming to earth. I know that you sympathize with my pain and loneliness. Hear my call, Jesus. Take my hand. It's in your name I pray, amen.

JOURNAL PROMPT: Why do you think God allows us to experience loneliness? How have you experienced God's love in times of loneliness?

Redeemed from Rejection

Reflect on God's Word

Have you ever endured rejection? Maybe you didn't get the job you wanted. Or a friend misunderstood you. Or worse, maybe your spouse or your children turned their backs on you.

You're in good company: Jesus also felt rejected and alone. The night before he died, he experienced great sorrow. In his distress, his sweat became drops of blood. Judas, one of his disciples, betrayed him and led the temple guards to arrest him. Can you imagine how painful that must have been? Jesus had spent hours and hours loving and teaching this man, and yet he turned against him. The next day, as Jesus was dying on the cross, he cried out, "My God, my God, why have you forsaken me?" (Mark 15:34).

With the sins of the world on his shoulders, Jesus became sin for us and therefore could not be looked upon by his holy heavenly Father. We know it was only temporary, that once his blood was shed, the penalty would be paid, but even momentary separation from God the Father would have been gut-wrenching for Jesus.

Because Jesus was willing to experience God's momentary rejection, he paved the way for your sins to be forgiven so you could be welcomed as a beloved child of your heavenly Father!

In Galatians 4:4–6 (ESV) we read, "But when the fullness of time had come, God sent forth his Son, born of woman, born under the law, to redeem those who were under the law, so that we might receive adoption as sons. And because you are sons, God has sent the Spirit of his Son into our hearts, crying, 'Abba! Father!'"

Did you catch that? You have received the Spirit of God in your heart. You have been adopted into God's family. You can now call God your daddy.

Imagine sitting under a tree with your heavenly Father. He sits next to you with his arm around you. A gentle breeze rustles through the branches above. Hear him tell you how much he loves you, how much you please him. You are the apple of his eye (Psalm 17:8). He delights in you (Psalm 18:19). He sings a love song to you (Zephaniah 3:17). He watches over you while you sleep and while you are awake (Psalm 3:5).

You openheartedly share with him your struggles and concerns. When you hesitate to reveal something, he lovingly urges you on. When you try to hide your face from him, he lifts up your head. You see only love in his eyes.

Your standing as a child of the King of Kings means you don't need to let the rejection of any human or the loneliness it may bring define you. Yes, it stings. Yes, it can be so very painful. The key in those times is to look into your Father's eyes and see his love for you. Your worth is not in what you can do, how attractive you are, or how much money you have. Your worth is completely in who you are: God's child.

Release Your Loneliness

Are you feeling the loneliness that comes from rejection? Take a deep breath. Slowly exhale. Feel the rejection leaving your body. Thank God that he understands your pain because Jesus was also rejected. Now inhale. Breathe in the love your heavenly Father has for you. Feel it surround you like a warm blanket. You have been adopted into his family. Feel how much he loves you. Feel his peace in your heart.

Search your heart. Can you feel the love of God, your Father, who chose you to be part of his family? Picture yourself receiving the Holy Spirit, the Spirit of adoption. Watch closely as the Holy Spirit takes your hand and puts it into the hand of God, your heavenly Father. You have been adopted into his family.

Spend a few minutes thinking about how much God loves you. Thank Jesus for suffering rejection during his life so you could become a part of a forever family. Thank him for paving the way for God to adopt you into his family.

Dear Father, thank you for sending Jesus to suffer rejection and loneliness on the cross to pay for my sins. Thank you for forgiving me and adopting me into your forever family. Today I receive your love. When I feel the sting of rejection, remind me you love me with perfect love. Open my heart and cause me to love you as my Abba, my Father. In the name of your Son, amen.

JOURNAL PROMPT: How has God comforted you during times of rejection and loneliness? Take a moment to write down your thoughts.

You Are Never Alone

Reflect on God's Word

When you're lost in the dark caverns of loneliness, it's easy to believe that you *are* alone and will *always* be alone, that you will always strain your eyes looking for a glimmer of light. You can easily believe that your suffering is meaningless and that your pain will keep you isolated forever.

But that's not the truth! God is always with you, and he is ready to comfort you.

When you are afflicted by loneliness, ponder these truths from Psalm 139:1–12:

> You have searched me, Lord,
>   and you know me.
> You know when I sit and when I rise;
>   you perceive my thoughts from afar.
> You discern my going out and my lying down;
>   you are familiar with all my ways.
> Before a word is on my tongue
>   you, Lord, know it completely.
> You hem me in behind and before,
>   and you lay your hand upon me.

Such knowledge is too wonderful for me,
    too lofty for me to attain.

Where can I go from your Spirit?
    Where can I flee from your presence?
If I go up to the heavens, you are there;
    if I make my bed in the depths, you are
        there.
If I rise on the wings of the dawn,
    if I settle on the far side of the sea,
even there your hand will guide me,
    your right hand will hold me fast.
If I say, "Surely the darkness will hide me
    and the light become night around me,"
even the darkness will not be dark to you;
    the night will shine like the day,
    for darkness is as light to you.

There's a big word that's used to describe this: omnipresent. Everywhere at one time. Isaiah 57:15 (ESV) says, "For thus says the One who is high and lifted up, who inhabits eternity, whose name is Holy: 'I dwell in the high and holy place, and also with him who is of a contrite and lowly spirit, to revive the spirit of the lowly, and to revive the heart of the contrite.'"

See yourself in your darkest moments and see God there with you. He himself says that he dwells with those who are humble and brought low. He revives their spirits and their hearts.

Think about your life and imagine God with you in every moment and every place. See yourself far away from everything you know and everyone you love. See God holding you even there. See yourself in the darkest place, and see God there, too, unafraid of the dark, shining his light on you.

Sometimes children who have no siblings will invent an imaginary friend. They play with that friend, have conversations with that friend, go everywhere with that friend right by their side. Sometimes we can feel like God is an imaginary friend because we can't see him. We can't feel his touch or hear his voice with our ears. It can begin to feel like he's not really there.

But faith is the assurance of things not seen (Hebrews 11:1). Even when we don't see God, he's there. Picture the trees blowing in the wind, their leaves fluttering and flying. You don't see the wind, but you see the effects of the wind, so you know it's there. We can't physically see gravity, but we feel its effects every day, especially when you drop something breakable on a tile floor. You don't think, "Oh, why did that happen?" You know it was because of gravitational pull.

The effects of God's presence with you are seen in the peace he gives you when you turn to him in prayer. They're seen in the provision of nature that speaks his name. Psalm 19:1 tells us, "The heavens declare the glory of God; the skies proclaim the work of his hands." Beauty, laughter, nature— all these things can remind you of the nearness of God.

When loneliness hits and you want to believe that you're

all alone, turn to the God who is near. His Spirit is living within you. Jesus himself told his disciples, "And I will ask the Father, and he will give you another advocate to help you and be with you forever—the Spirit of truth" (John 14:16–17).

You truly are never alone.

Release Your Loneliness

Now take a deep breath and slowly exhale. As you continue to practice breathing slowly and deeply, pay attention to your body, noticing where your sadness or loneliness has been residing. Where are you weighed down? In your shoulders, your chest, your back? Inhale into that part of your body, and as you exhale, feel yourself lighten a little. Let your breath comfort you.

It's okay to feel lonely. So in this moment, don't deny how you feel or try to pretend your way out of loneliness. Don't try to hide your feelings from God. Admit your deepest feelings to him and ask him to meet you in them, to reveal himself to you in them. Go outside at night and look at the stars, or during the day let the beauty of nature reflect to you the goodness of God.

Make it a point to see the effects of God's presence. How is he moving in the world right around you? And then see how he's moving in the world at large. Let that remind you of God's omnipresence. He is everywhere at one time, and he is with you all the time.

Can you let go of the lies that want to trap you today? Refuse to believe that God doesn't care. Refuse to believe that you are alone. Instead, hold on to these great, unchanging truths: God is with you; God loves you; God will comfort you in your loneliness.

Father of the heavenly lights, who does not change like shifting shadows, thank you for being with me in the darkness of my loneliness. I know that the darkness is not dark to you. I know that you can see me wherever I am and however I feel. Help me even in my loneliness to feel your presence and your comfort. Help me turn my eyes on you so I can see all you are doing in my life. Thank you for your love and presence in my life. I have faith that you are there even when I can't see you. I will hold your hand. In Jesus' name I pray, amen.

JOURNAL PROMPT: How can you remind yourself of God's presence when you find yourself feeling lonely? List some specific actions you can take, like taking a walk and praising God for his presence in creation or reading stories of his presence to others in the Bible.

PART 5

EVERYDAY CONCERNS

There Is Nothing God Cannot Handle

Reflect on God's Word

Imagine you're getting ready to hire a contractor to redo your bathroom. You research and decide to hire someone with a great reputation for finishing the work on time and on budget. As he begins his work, do you become anxious and worried about whether he will do a good job and meet your expectations? Probably not. Do you sit next to him and give him instructions about how you think things should be done? That would be ridiculous. You read testimony after testimony about how great his work is. You called in the expert, and now you let him do the job you hired him to do.

But do you sometimes treat God this way? Do you worry about whether he'll come through, keep his word, or be reliable? Do you give him suggestions about what to do in a given situation? More than a human contractor known for his good work, God can be trusted to care deeply about everything in your life and work for your good and his glory.

Philippians 4:6 (ESV) says, "Do not be anxious about anything, but in everything by prayer and supplication with thanksgiving let your requests be made known to God."

Think about those words *anything* and *everything*. You don't need to worry about *anything*; instead, God wants you to pray about *everything*. That's pretty all-inclusive, isn't it? God wants you to talk to him about big things and little things, and then let him be in control. He's the expert.

If God is God, you might think, *He already knows what I need, so why do I need to ask?* The answer is found in Philippians 4:7, which says, "And the peace of God, which transcends all understanding, will guard your hearts and your minds in Christ Jesus."

When we pray to the Lord and tell him what we need, his peace comes and guards our minds and hearts in Christ Jesus. Peace is something we need every day because anxiety often hits without warning and forces peace out. In the midst of hardship, worry seems to take over until you're overwhelmed and hopeless. But that's the perfect time to talk to God and roll all your worries onto him while thanking him for his peace and love.

Maybe your concern is getting to an appointment on time when there's more traffic than you anticipated. That may seem like a small thing that you don't want to bother God about, but he cares that your heart is at peace. He wants you to talk to him about it, and then he wants you to let him get you where you need to go. Maybe you will be late, but you will have peace in your heart.

Maybe your concern is on a much larger scale. Maybe you don't know how you're going to make your rent or mortgage payment because you've missed a lot of work due to illness. God has promised to supply all your needs according to the riches of his glory in Christ Jesus (Philippians 4:19). He wants you to talk to him about it. He knows your concerns, and he wants to give you his peace as you wait on him to supply your needs.

God is never bothered by your requests. Like a father who delights when his child comes to him with a request, God delights in hearing what you need. Hebrews 5:7–8 says, "During the days of Jesus' life on earth, he offered up prayers and petitions with fervent cries and tears to the one who could save him from death, and he was heard because of his reverent submission. Son though he was, he learned obedience from what he suffered." So how much more should we cry out to God during our times of need or suffering?

Maybe you complicate things, but the Worldwide English Version sure makes it simple: "Do not worry about anything. Talk to God about everything. Thank him for what you have. Ask him for what you need" (Philippians 4:6). When you have a need, do you tend to worry about it? Or do you ask God for help and trust him to take care of it?

Release Your Everyday Concerns

Take some deep, relaxing breaths. Breathe in God's peace and exhale any worry or anxiety you're feeling. Focus on the Lord's closeness and settle into his presence.

Now think about this question: How does bringing your requests to God help lessen your anxiety and worry during times of suffering?

When you ask God for help, you express your dependence on him instead of yourself, and then his peace surrounds you. Imagine a small child approaching a beloved parent. It doesn't matter how big or small the request is, the child approaches the parent with confidence, knowing they care and they are trustworthy.

If you feel worry or anxiety trying to pull you under, the best thing you can do is stop and pray. No matter where you are, reach out to the Lord and tell him how you feel and what you need. Thank him for always being there to hear your prayers.

Don't think you're bothering God with your small requests; no request is insignificant, and no prayer or petition is beyond his ability. It's your job to pray in faith; it's his job to answer.

When you combine your prayer and petitions with thankfulness for what God has done for you already, he hears you. When you remember what God has brought you through in the past, your faith increases.

Remember, by praying and bringing your requests to the Lord, you are admitting your dependence on him instead of yourself. This attitude of humility opens the door for God to move mightily on your behalf.

Dear God, I realize that sometimes I let worry and anxiety overwhelm me when I should be talking to you about my concerns. Help me remember that you hear me when I pray, you care about everything I'm going through, and I can trust you to keep your word. I choose to always have a thankful attitude whenever I make my requests to you. Instead of worrying, help me stop and talk to you about everything, no matter how big or small it is. I don't need to feel anxious about anything because you are reliable and trustworthy! Thank you for never letting me down. I know the plans you have for me are good! Amen.

JOURNAL PROMPT: How can you remind yourself to pray about everything instead of worrying? Journal about your most urgent requests and humbly bring them to the Lord.

Trusting God in Divorce

Reflect on God's Word

About twenty years ago on a bitterly cold midnight in Minnesota, a county park ranger knocked loudly on the window of a young pastor's van. Fresh from a broken marriage, with nowhere to go, the pastor was trying to sleep in his van that was parked just north of Minneapolis in this county park.

The park ranger said, "I'm sorry, this park is closed. You'll need to go somewhere else."

The pastor found himself driving around this large city searching for a quiet, safe spot to rest his eyes, if only for a few hours. Finally settling behind an office park, he curled up with a blanket and slept.

The next morning, he went to a YMCA to take a shower and get some coffee. This was his new normal, wandering in the desert, alone, in pain and desperate for a word from the Lord. He was a long, long way from the flock he had shepherded as a pastor. He was in serious need of a shepherd himself.

That was one of the worst seasons of this pastor's life. He was flooded with feelings of anger, fear, loneliness, and shame. As Christians who promised to be faithful "'til death do us part," it's devastating to be one of those Christian divorce statistics.

Maybe that's where you are now. You are brokenhearted, tired, hurt, angry, bitter, and confused.

It seems hard to believe that there can be joy through this devastating experience. Yet Jesus can bring joy alive during this time. The young pastor's strength to get through this divorce was rooted in the joy that comes from the Holy Spirit. While God can't take away the experience and disappointment of a divorce, through Jesus, the sting of it will eventually diminish in the presence of the kind of joy that only comes from him.

While each story of divorce is different, God knows your pain.

Divorce breaks the marriage covenant, a promise between you and your spouse and God. There's a reason God hates divorce: It's a broken promise, a rebellion against him. The Bible calls this *sin*.

When Christians talk about divorce, we often miss an important distinction: God hates *divorce*, not *the divorced*. God hates *sin*, not *sinners*. Jesus died for us in God's greatest act of love to his children while we were still sinners (Romans 5:8).

Churches and parishes usually do not know what to do with Christians going through divorce because they don't want to appear to endorse divorce.

Perhaps you desperately want and need the Lord, but church is the last place you want to be. Many there simply don't know how to meet you in your darkest hour.

Churches often shy away from, or even shun, the Christians in their own congregations who need Christian divorce recovery advice. The Bible tells us that God "heals the brokenhearted and binds up their wounds" (Psalm 147:3), but many churches ignore those who are brokenhearted because of divorce.

Psalm 119:50 says, "My comfort in my suffering is this: Your promise preserves my life."

In a divorce situation, shame can creep into your heart and mind. But the glory and beauty of Christianity is that we always have a chance to start fresh with a clean slate, and God covers us with his forgiveness and grace continually. Now that doesn't mean that it's okay to keep freely sinning, yet new mercies every morning is an awesome reality when seen through God's eyes of love.

Some often say that divorce feels like a death. Closure is fleeting, and wounds are deep. Many divorced people say that they would rather be widowed because death does not carry the social stigma and feelings of failure that divorce does. Unlike with a death, where there is a funeral and support from family and friends, the people getting a divorce often grieve all alone. If there are children involved, they may be confused and hurt.

Isaiah 61:7–10 is a beautiful passage of Scripture packed with the promises of God for those who need restoration.

> Instead of your shame
> you will receive a double portion,

and instead of disgrace
>> you will rejoice in your inheritance.
And so you will inherit a double portion in
>> your land,
>> and everlasting joy will be yours.

"For I, the LORD, love justice;
>> I hate robbery and wrongdoing.
In my faithfulness I will reward my people
>> and make an everlasting covenant
>>> with them.
Their descendants will be known among the
>> nations
>> and their offspring among the peoples.
All who see them will acknowledge
>> that they are a people the LORD has
>>> blessed."

I delight greatly in the LORD;
>> my soul rejoices in my God.

Restoration and a good harvest are promised by the Lord. Even when the cause of your divorce is sin on your part, God will not forsake you if you humbly acknowledge him.

Joel 2:25 says, "I will repay you for the years the locusts have eaten—the great locust and the young locust, the other locusts and the locust swarm—my great army that I sent among you."

Let's go back to that pastor in the van. God worked blessing after blessing in his life to bring him into a new, fruitful life of ministry. God restored to him a work that is helping thousands of people hear and follow the word of God. Long behind him are the days in the desert because he trusted God to be faithful to him as he gave his life into God's hands.

Maybe you think God is finished with you. You assume he can't use you anymore because you are divorced, you are "damaged goods." But that's not how God works. He brought Lazarus back to life, restoring him to his family (John 11), and he will restore you if you trust in him. God is in the business of redeeming the lost and restoring people to abundant life.

Release Your Everyday Concerns

Take a few deep breaths if you find that helpful. Feel the Holy Spirit indwelling you as you breathe in, and sin leaving you as you breathe out.

Now picture a field ripe for the harvest. Golden wheat blows gently in the breeze. The sun is shining without a cloud in the sky. You smile and sigh deeply. Life is good.

Suddenly, on the horizon you see a low, dark cloud approaching. You shade your eyes to try to see what it is. It's not a storm. It's way too low. And then you hear a strange, low humming noise. It gets closer and closer until you finally realize what it is. Locusts. Thousands upon thousands of locusts. And they are tearing through your harvest and leaving only destruction in their wake.

Does that feel like your life? It's devastating to see all you worked hard to build ruined in one fell swoop.

Take another deep breath. Hold it for a moment, and then release it.

In your mind, turn around and see another field, this one twice as big as the former, bearing twice the amount of grain. Watch as the harvester comes and reaps all that beautiful golden grain. The harvester is God. That field is the life he wants to give you. Trust him to do more than you could ask or imagine in your life after divorce.

God is a restorer. He is a redeemer. As you give him lordship over your life, you will see it renewed.

Lord, I know that you hate divorce, and I'm so sorry for the role I played in causing the end of my marriage. But I'm so grateful for your love. Restore to me the joy of my salvation. Restore to me the years the locusts have eaten. Restore to me the work of my hands for your kingdom. I want to follow you wholeheartedly. I want to do what you want me to do. I don't presume upon your grace, but I desperately need it. It's in the redeeming name of Jesus that I pray, amen.

JOURNAL PROMPT: Write out some of the names of God (Healer, Redeemer, and so on). What evidence of these characteristics of God have you seen in your life? Does that help you lean on him for the future?

God Is Able to Take Care of Your Future

Reflect on God's Word

According to the American Psychological Association, "Stress about money and finances appears to have a significant impact on Americans' lives. Nearly three-quarters (72 percent) of adults report feeling stressed about money at least some of the time and nearly one-quarter say that they experience extreme stress about money (22 percent rate their stress about money during the past month as an 8, 9 or 10 on a 10-point scale). In some cases, people are even putting their health care needs on hold because of financial concerns."[1]

Everyday life can bring anxiety about finances, and advancing years can increase that if you fear you won't have enough to live on after you retire. Maybe you were really good about creating retirement savings when you were younger, but there can be lingering fears that your situation will require resources you don't feel you have.

In the Sermon on the Mount, Jesus spoke to the crowds about not laying up treasures on earth or being afraid of what you will eat or drink or what you will wear. He wraps up that topic with this verse in Matthew 6:34: "Therefore do not worry about tomorrow, for tomorrow will worry about itself. Each day has enough trouble of its own."

Jesus was not being trite or brushing off the people's concerns when he spoke those words. It was a true statement he wanted his listeners to hear. He will take care of your tomorrows. It's a promise.

Isaiah 41:10 (ESV) says, "Fear not, for I am with you; be not dismayed, for I am your God; I will strengthen you, I will help you, I will uphold you with my righteous right hand."

Some days it's a moment-by-moment decision to put your fears into the hands of the Lord. And that's okay. He's always there by your side. But he does not want you to worry. He really will take care of you, even if you can't see how. We often try to figure out how God might work things out, but God is not constrained by our finite minds. Give God permission to surprise you with his answers to your prayers.

This story is told about nineteenth-century missionary George Müller, who served as a coordinator of orphanages in Bristol, England:

> One morning, all the plates and cups and bowls on the table were empty. There was no food in the larder and no money to buy food. The children were standing, waiting for their morning meal, when Müller said, "Children, you know we must be in time for school." Then lifting up his hands he prayed, "Dear Father, we thank Thee for what Thou art going to give us to eat."
>
> There was a knock at the door. The baker stood

there, and said, "Mr. Müller, I couldn't sleep last night. Somehow I felt you didn't have bread for breakfast, and the Lord wanted me to send you some. So I got up at 2 a.m. and baked some fresh bread, and have brought it."

Mr. Müller thanked the baker, and no sooner had he left, when there was a second knock at the door. It was the milkman. He announced that his milk cart had broken down right in front of the orphanage, and he would like to give the children his cans of fresh milk so he could empty his wagon and repair it.[2]

Now, miracles like this don't happen often, but there are stories upon stories of people who needed a specific amount of money, and an anonymous gift would show up in their mailbox. But sometimes, help comes from organizations specifically geared toward meeting the needs of those who find themselves in financial difficulty.

Let's spend a little more time in Isaiah 41:17–20. These words were spoken to the nation of Israel, but God does not change, and so his words are true for you today.

"The poor and needy search for water,
　　but there is none;
　　their tongues are parched with thirst.
But I the LORD will answer them;
　　I, the God of Israel, will not
　　　　forsake them.
I will make rivers flow on barren heights,

and springs within the valleys.
I will turn the desert into pools of water,
and the parched ground into springs.
I will put in the desert
the cedar and the acacia, the myrtle and
the olive.
I will set junipers in the wasteland,
the fir and the cypress together,
so that people may see and know,
may consider and understand,
that the hand of the LORD has done this,
that the Holy One of Israel has created it."

God is not hampered by your bank account. His provision for you will be perfect.

Release Your Everyday Concerns

Take a deep breath. Hold your hands open to the Lord to show him you are willing to let go of your fear and trust him to provide.

Keep taking slow, deep breaths as you release your anxiety to the Lord. See only the face of the Lord as he tells you how much he loves you.

Feel the hands of God holding you up, staying with you, not letting you fall. Rest in that security for a few moments.

Can you trust God to provide in unexpected ways? There's a silly tale about a man caught in a flood that might bring some of this home:

A fellow was stuck on his rooftop in a flood. He was praying to God for help. Soon a man in a rowboat came by and the fellow shouted to the man on the roof, "Jump in, I can save you."

The stranded fellow shouted back, "No, it's OK, I'm praying to God and he is going to save me." So the rowboat went on.

Then a motorboat came by. The fellow in the motorboat shouted, "Jump in, I can save you."

To this the stranded man said, "No thanks, I'm praying to God and he is going to save me. I have faith." So the motorboat went on.

Then a helicopter came by and the pilot shouted down, "Grab this rope and I will lift you to safety."

To this the stranded man again replied, "No thanks, I'm praying to God and he is going to save me. I have faith." So the helicopter reluctantly flew away.

Soon the water rose above the rooftop and the man drowned. He went to Heaven. He finally got his chance to discuss this whole situation with God, at which point he exclaimed, "I had faith in you but you didn't save me, you let me drown. I don't understand why!"

To this God replied, "I sent you a rowboat and a motorboat and a helicopter, what more did you expect?"[3]

Has God been trying to send you rescue from your financial situation and you've missed it? You may not see something as a way out of your financial situation, but God sometimes makes a way that is unexpected or looks different from what you imagined.

Ask the Holy Spirit to reveal to you where you have not been trusting God to provide for you. Confess that to him and let his forgiveness and grace wash over you. He understands and he cares. He will not hold your sin against you. He lovingly wants to lead you to trust him completely.

Do you really believe that God will take care of you? Let the words of Jesus resonate: "Do not worry about tomorrow" (Matthew 6:34). Determine today to live one day at a time through the power of the Holy Spirit.

Lord God, I know in my mind that you will provide for me, but my heart sometimes needs help catching up. Today I give you my fears about my financial future. Help me look to your Word instead of the world for what is true about money. Help me trust you completely and not let the condition of my finances cause me to be anxious. Today has enough trouble of its own. Help me not to worry about what tomorrow will bring. I want to honor you in all things. Your words are true. I believe that you will provide for me. Help my unbelief. It's in the name of Jesus that I pray, amen.

JOURNAL PROMPT: Write out what your fears for the future are. What about God's character helps you to know that he will meet your needs?

When Your Job Weighs You Down

Reflect on God's Word

The hit television show *Undercover Boss* puts company CEOs in situations where they are interacting, while disguised, with actual employees in their company. Many times it features a disgruntled franchise employee who doesn't know they're interacting with the big boss, which can get them into big trouble if their attitude is bad or their work is shoddy. But sometimes it features an employee who is doing the best job they can do and treating anyone—even the unknown newcomer who is actually the boss—like they're the most important person in the world.

It's an interesting premise: Do you do the best job you can no matter who you're working with or who you're serving? Or do you complain to your coworkers or even slack off when the boss isn't around?

Colossians 3:23–24 says, "Whatever you do, work at it with all your heart, as working for the Lord, not for human masters, since you know that you will receive an inheritance from the Lord as a reward. It is the Lord Christ you are serving."

Work is one of the most common causes of stress in

the United States.[4] From long hours to low wages to high demands, jobs can take a toll on our health. Finding ways to combat this stress is essential. So what does "working for the Lord" look like?

First of all, trust in the Lord's provision is essential. Do you believe that your job was provided by God, or did you get it by your own efforts? If you took the job you currently have knowing it might not be a good fit, but it was all you could find, consider asking God to provide you with something that would better meet your needs. But in the meantime, while you are there, give it your all. Be a diligent and dedicated worker, knowing that ultimately, God is your boss.

If you are in a high-pressure job that is stealing your joy, time with your family, and your health, even if it means adjusting your lifestyle and making less money, consider scaling back or finding something different that will allow you to focus on the things that are most important: your faith, your family, and your health. Working for the Lord does not mean working your fingers to the bone and putting your health at risk. It means dedicating what you do to him and letting him lead and guide you in your job.

Maybe you simply could find no other job, but this one is not providing you with enough money to pay your bills. God sees you and he cares. He will meet your needs in ways that you can't imagine. Jesus said in Matthew 7:7–11, "Ask and it will be given to you; seek and you will find; knock and the door will be opened to you. For everyone who asks receives;

the one who seeks finds; and to the one who knocks, the door will be opened. Which of you, if your son asks for bread, will give him a stone? Or if he asks for a fish, will give him a snake? If you, then, though you are evil, know how to give good gifts to your children, how much more will your Father in heaven give good gifts to those who ask him!"

God is not an "undercover boss." He is right out front telling you that he's the one you're serving with your work. But he will always be a fair and kind boss, treating everyone with love and justice. You might not feel that way in your current job. But how you approach your work, the value you find in it, can make a difference.

When you were hired, you were hired for a certain job. Let's take restaurant work, for example. Maybe you were hired to be a dishwasher. That's a very important job. If dishes and utensils and pots and pans aren't washed, cooking and serving could not be done. It's not a glamorous job, to be sure, but it's necessary for the working of the restaurant. How you do your job will make an impression on those around you and may even point someone to Christ.

Or maybe you were hired to be a server. It's definitely hard work, and sometimes you have to put up with grouchy and demanding people. But it's an important job in the food-service business. You might look at your manager and see that they make a lot more money than you do for what appears to be work that isn't as hard as yours. Or maybe you feel like they're doing a terrible job. How you're treated may cause you to desire to do a less-than-stellar job. Your response to your situation, the attitude of servanthood you bring, can show people that your dependence is on Christ.

God wants you to thrive in your workplace just as he does in every other part of your life. If things are less than satisfactory to you, consider where that dissatisfaction stems from. Talk to your heavenly Father about your job. And then listen to what he has to say to you.

Remember, when you ask for wisdom and believe he will give it, God will bring clarity to your situation. He cares about you and what you do for a living. Work for him and let him provide for your needs.

Release Your Everyday Concerns

As you think about your job situation, exhale any frustrations or stress you might be feeling about your job. The Lord is with you as you work. As you relate to your coworkers, he is your confidence. As you worry about making ends meet, he is your provider. As you struggle to find your place, he is your home.

Spend some time seeking the wisdom of God about your job. As you seek the Lord's will concerning life at work, ask him if there is anything you need to do differently.

Perhaps you need to focus more on pleasing the Lord and not man, being satisfied with the job you have instead of desiring someone else's. Or perhaps you need to ask God to provide another job.

Whatever the issue, quietly seek the Lord's will for several moments.

How can you positively affect your workplace by considering God to be your boss?

Remember, you are valuable in the workplace. When you focus on working for the Lord, doing the job that he has given you to do, you will have a greater sense of peace and satisfaction.

Gracious God, thank you for being with me in the workplace. When my job is stressful, help me know you are there. Please give me your peace that surpasses all understanding. I ask for unity with my coworkers and the understanding of my employer. Help me remember that, ultimately, I work for you. Help me have the heart of a servant, but also help me know when it's time to make a change. Thank you for your Word that reminds me that you are my provider, and you will give me the work you want me to do. I pray these things in Jesus' name, amen.

JOURNAL PROMPT: If you feel overwhelmed by your job situation, please know you are not alone. Write down your concerns to the Lord and know that he cares about you. You are valuable to him, and he will guide your steps.

Same God in an Uncertain World

Reflect on God's Word

The year 2020 changed people's lives. Day by day everything around us changed because of the world's efforts to stem the tide of Covid-19. Stores closed, people lost jobs, curfews were imposed, stay-at-home orders were invoked. It was a scary and anxious time. We asked ourselves, *How long will businesses and schools be closed? How long will we have to isolate ourselves from others? How long before life can get back to normal?* Uncertainty seemed to be the order of the day.

But this one thing remained: "Jesus Christ is the same yesterday and today and forever" (Hebrews 13:8).

No matter what happens today, tomorrow, or a year from now, Jesus Christ, God incarnate, is the same yesterday, today, and forever.

How wonderful it is to know that Jesus, the second person of the Trinity, the only begotten Son of God, very God of very God, creator of the universe, never ever changes.

James 1:17 says, "Every good and perfect gift is from above, coming down from the Father of the heavenly lights, who does not change like shifting shadows."

BibleRef.com says, "James urges us to flip the typical

human script. He calls us to make a new list: all the good things we do have. Where did all those good things come from? James is encouraging believers in Christ to tell themselves the truth: God gave you every single good thing in your life. He is the source of all the good you have and all the good you crave. Who God is does not change when our circumstances change. He doesn't go from being a good God to a bad God when our trials begin. He is still the source of all the good in our lives. He never changes."[5]

In Exodus 3:14, God tells Moses, "I AM WHO I AM. This is what you are to say to the Israelites: 'I AM has sent me to you.'" God always existed, he is holy and perfect, and there is nothing about him that changes, because he has no need of anything.

In Malachi 3:6, God says of himself: "I the LORD do not change. So you, the descendants of Jacob, are not destroyed."

And Psalm 102:25–27 says, "In the beginning you laid the foundations of the earth, and the heavens are the work of your hands. They will perish, but you remain; they will all wear out like a garment. Like clothing you will change them and they will be discarded. But you remain the same, and your years will never end."

When faced with uncertain times, it might be your default to think God has left the world unattended, like a parent who leaves their toddler to their own devices. Every parent knows that chaos ensues when that happens. But God does not leave us. He has promised to never leave us or forsake us (Deuteronomy 31:6).

Unfortunately, we are all born into a fallen world. Disease, death, and destruction are just givens in a sinful world. When we expect everything will run smoothly, we are bound for disappointment.

James 1:12 says, "Blessed is the one who perseveres under trial because, having stood the test, that person will receive the crown of life that the Lord has promised to those who love him."

Take heart! Even as you face uncertainty, keep your eyes on Jesus because not only has he promised you the crown of life when you have stood the test of time, he is also the one constant you can count on through it all.

Release Your Everyday Concerns

Take a long, deep breath and rest in the truth that God never changes. No matter how uncertain life is, you can always depend on God being the same.

Thank the Lord for being unchangeable and for being your strong anchor in this tumultuous sea we call life.

As you come before God today, lay aside your concerns and your need to know what's going to happen tomorrow, and just sit at his feet, resting in the knowledge that you can trust him because you know who he is. Ask God to show you from his Word the truth about his character and his love that has never changed. That there is no variation or shifting shadow in him. Thank him for what he shows you about himself.

God is not afraid of your emotions. Give to him your

sorrow over the things happening in the world, your fear about how things are going to turn out, and all your what-ifs.

What do you know to be true about Jesus today, in the midst of turmoil and uncertainty? Is he still good? Is he still loving? Is he still powerful? Focus today on Jesus instead of all that is in chaos around you. He is your anchor. He is your solid rock.

Jesus, you are the Alpha and the Omega, the one who was, who is, and who is to come. I praise you for being the one thing I can count on in this ever-changing world. I love you and praise you today because I can always count on you. You have always been just, you have always been merciful, you have always been kind, generous, and loving. And I know you always and forever will be. On you, the solid rock, I stand. All other ground is sinking sand. In our uncertain world, you are my certainty. In your solid, unchanging name I pray, amen.

JOURNAL PROMPT: Write down the things you know were true about God yesterday. Acknowledge to him that you know those things are still true today.

PART 6

SHAME

Completely Saved

Reflect on God's Word

Does shame ever keep you from truly believing that Jesus is able to forgive you? Do you fear that your sins are too many or too egregious?

Maybe sins you committed yesterday keep nipping at your heels like an angry dog, refusing to let you go, and you find yourself pulled backward into shame and regret. Maybe failures from decades ago, when remembered, still have the power to draw you down into despair.

Though you may have trouble moving forward and forgiving yourself, God doesn't have any trouble doing that. He has forgiven you completely. Your sins and failures can't keep you from God. You are completely saved.

Hebrews 7:25 says of Christ, "Therefore he is able to save completely those who come to God through him, because he always lives to intercede for them."

What a beautiful verse! It really contains every aspect of the gospel message for us. Jesus is *able* to save. Not *might* be able to save, but *can* save! And when he saves, he does it completely, once and for always. He is able to do this because he sits next to the Father as our advocate, interceding with God on our behalf. Amazing!

John 10:28 says that nothing and no one can pluck us out of the hand of God. Picture yourself securely in the hand of God—forever, completely, perfectly, and for eternity.

In 1 John 2:1–2, the apostle John writes, "My dear children, I write this to you so that you will not sin. But if anybody does sin, we have an advocate with the Father—Jesus Christ, the Righteous One. He is the atoning sacrifice for our sins, and not only for ours but also for the sins of the whole world."

That word *advocate* describes someone similar to an intercessor, someone taking up for you when you can't do something yourself. Courts have advocates for children who are in unstable or dangerous situations. Called a "guardian *ad litem*," these people are appointed by the court to represent the best interests of the child.

And then there's the term *atoning sacrifice*. Jesus assumed the punishment for our sin. He took our place. He intruded into the courtroom and paid the debt we owed. He covered it. Picture that in your mind. See Jesus physically covering you, protecting you, shielding you from the effects of sin and judgment. He reconciled us to God by dying on the cross for our sins because Scripture says in Leviticus 17:11, "For the life of a creature is in the blood, and I have given it to you to make atonement for yourselves on the altar; it is the blood that makes atonement for one's life." And Hebrews 9:22, referring to the verse in Leviticus, says, "In fact, the law requires that nearly everything be cleansed with blood, and without the shedding of blood there is no forgiveness."

How do you respond to the truth that no matter what you have done, Jesus has exchanged places with you? He took your sins on himself, and he paid the penalty for everything you have done or will do.

Psalm 103:12 (ESV) says, "As far as the east is from the west, so far does he remove our transgressions from us."

So how far exactly *is* the east from the west? That line extends for eternity. God has removed your sins and thrown them so far away that they can never be found. The accuser can never use them against you. Imagine the devil trying to accuse you of sin. He comes up empty. Your sins cannot be found.

You are in Christ's saving grip, and nothing is strong enough to tear you out of his hands.

Release Your Shame

Take a deep breath, hold it for a moment, and then let it out slowly. As your breath leaves your body, feel your shame being blown away. Feel your body relax. Still your mind and your heart.

Spend time now thanking God for his plan to save you and to bring you back into relationship with him by his grace, through faith in his Son.

Picture a balloon that over your lifetime has been blown up by all of the shame you have ever felt. Maybe it's the things you've done. Maybe it's things others have done to you. That balloon holds every harsh and demeaning word, every tear, every dark thought. You've been carrying that balloon around with you like a child in the park. Looking at it, holding on to it, believing all that it holds.

Now picture God taking that balloon and poking a hole in it. Even as you watch, everything that balloon held flows out of it. Soon there is nothing left to hold that balloon up. Now watch as God breathes new life into that balloon. All the holes and weak spots seal, and it lifts higher and higher, grows bigger and more beautiful, until it is like a glorious hot-air balloon, filled with God's glory, his forgiveness, and his grace.

Do this now: Cup your hands softly, now grip them together tightly. Imagine your life, your soul, being forever locked into the soft, tender, loving, protecting hands of Jesus. You are completely and forever saved. That new life in you can never be taken away.

Dear God of good news, I accept these words you have given as a gift today and every day. Give me the humility and courage to accept that you, Christ Jesus, are able to save me forever, completely, perfectly, and for eternity. Thank you for loving me. Thank you for calling me to yourself and giving me a desire for you. And thank you for living to intercede and intervene on my behalf before the Father. In your precious name I pray, amen.

JOURNAL PROMPT: What has been filling your balloon? With the help of the Holy Spirit, list those things that have brought you shame. Don't be afraid. Jesus is right there by your side. When you are done, in bold letters, write the word *FORGIVEN* over the entire list.

Completely Loved

Reflect on God's Word

Nickolas Ashford and Valerie Simpson wrote a song in 1966 called "Ain't No Mountain High Enough." It was recorded and made popular by Marvin Gaye and Tammi Terrell in 1967, and again in 1970 when it was recorded by Diana Ross. The idea is a simple one: nothing can keep us from the one we love.

It's romantic to think that someone would love us so much that nothing could keep them from getting to us when we need them. Well, humanly speaking, that's probably not possible, but it *is* possible with God.

Consider Romans 8:38–39: "For I am convinced that neither death nor life, neither angels nor demons, neither the present nor the future, nor any powers, neither height nor depth, nor anything else in all creation, will be able to separate us from the love of God that is in Christ Jesus our Lord."

When regrets threaten to consume you, or when you are dealing with the unavoidable results of sin in your life, take comfort in the truth that nothing can separate you from God's love.

The story of the prophet Hosea and his wife, Gomer,

gives us a powerful picture of how much God loves us. Israel had been unfaithful to God. They were worshiping false gods and had turned their backs on the one true God. So God directed Hosea to marry Gomer, a prostitute. God knew Gomer would be unfaithful to Hosea, just as Israel had been unfaithful to him.

And sure enough, Gomer left and went back to her former life of prostitution. And Hosea went after her and took her back. Hosea 3:1 says, "The LORD said to me, 'Go, show your love to your wife again, though she is loved by another man and is an adulteress. Love her as the LORD loves the Israelites, though they turn to other gods and love the sacred raisin cakes.'"

Not only did Hosea take Gomer back after her unfaithfulness, he bought her at a great price (Hosea 3:2).

Hosea showed great mercy to Gomer to illustrate God's great love and mercy toward Israel. He was a living illustration of God's love and faithfulness.

The world may not be merciful, but God is always merciful. God does not deal harshly with you. Instead, he loves you. In fact, his steadfast love for those who fear him is as high as the heavens are above the earth. Do you know how far it is from where you are to the farthest reaches of the galaxy? Imagine God's love reaching even further than that.

Our heavenly Father is an all-powerful God, whose love extends beyond the reach of your imagination.

Today, don't let your regrets define you; rather, let the truth define you. And the truth is that in Christ, you are wholly forgiven and perfectly loved. Your sins are not too big for God.

Release Your Shame

Attend now to your breath, inhaling slowly, holding it, and then exhaling slowly. As you continue this slow, steady breathing, hold your hands open, palms down, as if you were dropping the regret and shame you've been carrying. Then flip your palms up, ready to receive the perfect love of God. Breathe slowly and expectantly, listening for God.

Your sins and wanderings from God may have consequences, but losing his love will *never* be one of them. Nothing can separate you from his love.

Let the reality of God's love infiltrate your heart. Rest in his presence. Your past failures do not define you. God wants to abide with you today. He wants you to know that what matters most is your identity in Jesus.

As you find comfort in the God of love, take a moment to praise him. Bless his name. Thank him now for the specific ways he has shown love to you.

God, you are gracious and compassionate, slow to anger and abounding in love. Thank you for forgiving me, redeeming me, and crowning me with your love and mercy. Please help me believe the truth that your love is more powerful than my sins. Help me to live in the freedom you offer rather than living trapped in regret. I ask this in the name of Jesus, amen.

JOURNAL PROMPT: Journal about the ways in which you have been unfaithful to God. How has he then showed his great love and faithfulness to you?

Completely Holy

Reflect on God's Word

Shame can rob us of joy, and it can harm our relationship with God and others.

Do you know what God thinks about your feelings of shame? He wants you to be free of them. He wants to make you holy.

Colossians 1:21–22 says, "Once you were alienated from God and were enemies in your minds because of your evil behavior. But now he has reconciled you by Christ's physical body through death to present you holy in his sight, without blemish and free from accusation."

When you're accused of something, shame can fall on you. Maybe you hear the words in your head: *You're lazy! You're a liar! You'll never amount to anything! How can God love you after what you've done?* Now take all those thoughts running through your mind and erase them. Instead, hear the soothing voice of God saying, "I love you, I have bought you at a price, I have freed you from your sins, and you are holy and blameless in my sight" (1 Corinthians 6:20, Revelation 1:5, Ephesians 1:4).

Remember that your reconciliation to God is not a

future event. It has already happened! You can stand today in his presence with confidence because of Christ's work on the cross.

God sees you as someone without a blemish, as someone who is free from accusation, all because of the work of Christ on the cross. Satan, on the other hand, wants you to feel shame. Don't let the devil rob you of joy. If you have made Jesus Lord of your life, then you are wearing the righteousness of Christ!

As you relax and meditate on God's grace and righteousness, take a deep breath and inhale God's peace.

God sees you as *holy*. *Blameless*. On her website Worth beyond Rubies, Diane Shirlaw-Ferreira says,

> In the Greek language, the word "blameless" is *amōmos* and it means, according to Strong's Exhaustive Concordance: *without blemish, as a sacrifice without spot or blemish morally: without blemish, faultless, unblameable.*
>
> How amazing is it that the word blameless used here is the same word used to describe a perfect sacrifice? It is the same word that describes Yeshua which makes sense because in the eyes of Almighty God He sees us through Him! When He looks at us, He sees us through the lens of Yeshua!"[1]

Have you ever known someone who constantly reminded you of the bad things you did? God does not do that. It's as if you've never committed a sin in your life—all because of the death, burial, and resurrection of Jesus. Though others may keep a record of your wrongs, you are blameless in the sight of the only One who really matters: your heavenly Father.

Satan wants to spoil your life with thoughts of shame and regret. God, though, wipes your sin-filled record clean, clothes you with his righteousness, and then places you on a path to heaven, where you will spend eternity with him.

Release Your Shame

When you have lived a long time in the shadow of shame, stepping into the light can be hard. So take a deep, cleansing breath. Take a few more if you need them. Feel your heart rate slow and your mind become steadier.

Now whisper, "Because of Christ, I am holy. I am blameless. I am without fault."

Thank God for this indescribable gift. As you keep breathing slowly, imagine yourself exhaling the shame and guilt that weighs you down. Open your palms to the heavens, as if you're receiving the Lord's blessings.

Isaiah 61:10 says God has clothed you with "garments of salvation" and arrayed you "in a robe of his righteousness."

Now imagine taking off a filthy, smelly garment that represents your sin. Next, imagine Jesus standing beside you and handing you a beautiful white robe that he insists you wear. "This is yours to wear *forever*," he says. "It represents the way I see you."

How does that new garment look on you?

Let this image linger in your mind and remind you that

because of Christ, you are holy and blameless in the presence of God. You have no reason to feel shame.

Take another deep breath, slowly exhale, and whisper to God, "Thank you."

> Dear Father, there is no one like you. You are righteous; you are holy. You are the God of grace, mercy, and peace. Your love never ends. Thank you for loving me. Thank you for giving me a second chance. Thank you for clothing me in the righteousness of Christ. Father, I ask that you guard my heart against feelings of shame and guilt. Help me cast the care of shame on you. Help me see myself the way you see me. It's in the name of Jesus that I pray, amen.

JOURNAL PROMPT: Write down some things God says about you, like "I have loved you with an everlasting love" (Jeremiah 31:3), or "While you were still a sinner, Christ died for you" (Romans 5:8). Fill the page with as many truths as you can think of. Let the Holy Spirit bring them to mind.

Completely Free

Reflect on God's Word

Can you imagine being a prisoner, freed by presidential pardon, but still living in your small, dark cell? As a follower of Jesus, if you still live under a veil of shame, you can easily understand how that prisoner might feel.

As psychologist Anna I. Smith says, "Shame makes us feel small."[2] And when we feel small, we don't feel like we can change. We can't move forward. We're bound by what we think we've done wrong.

Picture Jesus meeting the Gadarene man possessed by a legion of demons as told in Mark 5:1–4: "They went across the lake to the region of the Gerasenes. When Jesus got out of the boat, a man with an impure spirit came from the tombs to meet him. This man lived in the tombs, and no one could bind him anymore, not even with a chain. For he had often been chained hand and foot, but he tore the chains apart and broke the irons on his feet. No one was strong enough to subdue him."

Alone, isolated, feared, condemned. That's how shame makes you feel. Like you can't be seen. Though he constantly broke out of his chains because of his great strength, the man's soul was in complete bondage. "Night and day among the tombs and in the hills he would cry out and cut himself with stones" (Mark 5:5). Until Jesus set him free.

"As Jesus was getting into the boat, the man who had been demon-possessed begged to go with him. Jesus did not let him, but said, 'Go home to your own people and tell them how much the Lord has done for you, and how he has had mercy on you.' So the man went away and began to tell in the Decapolis how much Jesus had done for him. And all the people were amazed" (Mark 5:18–20).

Once the man had been freed of his possessing demons, he told everyone how he had been set free. He proclaimed Jesus throughout the area, and everyone was amazed.

Shame keeps you from living a life full of joy. It weighs you down and haunts your dreams. It causes you to doubt all you have been given in Christ. But you don't have to live this way. Christ has freed you—completely.

Galatians 5:1 says, "It is for freedom that Christ has set us free. Stand firm, then, and do not let yourselves be burdened again by a yoke of slavery." Paul was talking about the Galatians being guilted into being circumcised, to be slaves again to the law. Maybe you have felt shame heaped upon you because you were brought up in a legalistic church, made to believe that you had to follow all the rules. Paul is encouraging the Galatians, and you, to live in the freedom that Christ gave you when he died on the cross for your sins.

This freedom was not given so that you may do whatever you want (Galatians 5:13), but so that you wouldn't let yourself be shackled to the chains of shame that come when others set expectations on you that God never intended.

Romans 6:20–23 is another beautiful passage about freedom: "When you were slaves to sin, you were free from the control of righteousness. What benefit did you reap at that time from the things you are now ashamed of? Those things result in death! But now that you have been set free from sin and have become slaves of God, the benefit you reap leads to holiness, and the result is eternal life. For the wages of sin is death, but the gift of God is eternal life in Christ Jesus our Lord."

There is no joy in a jail cell, beaten and battered. Christ has set you free, so jump off that jail bed, push open that unlocked door, and leap into your freedom, proclaiming to all who will listen what Christ has done for you!

Release Your Shame

Take a deep breath and let it out slowly. Feel the tension release from your neck and shoulders. Open your arms wide, signifying that you have no shackles on your wrists. You have been set free.

John 8:36 says, "So if the Son sets you free, you will be free indeed."

Take a few more relaxing, peaceful, centering breaths. Get comfortable and settle into wherever you are. Become aware of God. Seek his presence, his freedom.

The Amplified Bible expands the meaning of Galatians 5:1 this way: "It was for this freedom that Christ set us free [completely liberating us]; therefore keep standing firm and do not be subject again to a yoke of slavery [which you once removed]."

Wrap yourself in these two words: *liberated* and *removed*. See yourself as completely *liberated* with your chains *removed*. What does that look like in your life today? Tomorrow? Next year?

Guilt brings with it the purpose of repentance. Shame, however, only holds you down. And shame does not come from God. He identifies you as a child of the King of Kings through the lens of the cross. He has completely removed your sin and your identity as a sinner. Guilt calls you to go forward in a different direction. Shame keeps you cowering, unwilling to see or be seen.

If you find yourself replaying hurtful and wrong things you have done, struggling with feelings of guilt and shame, you are living as if you are still shackled to shame.

Luke 4:18 tells us that Jesus said, "The Spirit of the Lord is on me, because he has anointed me to proclaim good news to the poor. He has sent me to proclaim freedom for the prisoners and recovery of sight for the blind, to set the oppressed free."

Jesus lived and died so you could be free from the bonds of sin and shame, so don't stay in those chains by rehashing what you have done or listening to the condemning voices of others. You are completely free.

Dear heavenly Father, sometimes feelings of shame crush me. When shame begins to define me, it binds me so I can't move. But I know shame is not from you. Lift it from me. Release my chains of shame over things I've done or things that have been done to me. I know your death on the cross transferred my sin to you, and I know you consider me forgiven, pure, perfect, and righteous. I know it was for freedom that Christ set me free, completely liberating me. Help me to not be subject again to the heavy weight of sin that Jesus removed once and for always on the cross. Let me live with peace, rest, and joy. It's in the name of Jesus that I pray, amen.

JOURNAL PROMPT: What word picture describes the freedom you have in Christ—the release of sin and your new identity in Christ? When did you first discover this new identity? And how do you hang on to this new identity?

From Prisoner to Partner

Reflect on God's Word

What do you do when shame threatens to overwhelm you? Maybe you've tried everything you can think of to get out from underneath it, but nothing seems to work. Whether you feel shame from what others have said or done to you or from decisions you have made, God wants to transform your pain and shame and use it for his purposes.

Maybe you wonder how your story can bring God glory. But God can use whatever has brought you shame and transform it into something that will give him honor. He can turn your pain into purpose.

Consider the story of the Samaritan woman at the well in John 4. Jesus was sitting by the well by himself because his disciples had gone into town to buy something to eat. It was about noon, and a woman from the town came to draw water. It was very unusual for a woman to come at that hour to draw water. That errand was usually done in the morning when it was cool.

Jesus proceeded to have quite a lengthy conversation with this woman about water and thirsting, but below the surface, Jesus was preparing to transform this woman's life.

Confronting her with the fact that she had been married to five different men and was currently living with a man to whom she was not married—a fact that would have caused her great shame in her society—Jesus revealed himself to her as the Messiah. Her response? "Then, leaving her water jar, the woman went back to the town and said to the people, 'Come, see a man who told me everything I ever did. Could this be the Messiah?'" (John 4:29).

This woman, who lived under a veil of shame because of the choices she had made and possibly circumstances that had been thrust upon her, had become a partner in declaring the good news of the Messiah.

Don't let shame make you deaf to the whispers of the Lord and his plans for you. You are completely saved, completely loved, completely holy, completely free. Deliverance from shame's oppression opens your ears to hear what God has planned for you.

Imagine for a few moments what it feels like to go from a prisoner to a partner with God.

Chuck Colson was a central figure in the Watergate scandal of the 1970s. He went to prison for his actions. After serving seven months in federal prison, Colson founded Prison Fellowship, the largest Christian nonprofit organization in the United States ministering to prisoners, former prisoners, and their families.[3] From prisoner to partner.

Nicky Cruz—warlord of a violent gang on the streets of New York in the 1950s, victim of severe child abuse, and considered a lost cause by the courts—gave his life to Jesus after encountering evangelist David Wilkerson. He went on to found Nicky Cruz Outreach and preach the good news of Jesus to youth around the world.[4] From prisoner to partner.

There is no life so lost that it cannot be found by Jesus. There is no soul so dark that the light of Jesus cannot shine in it. God wants to use you in his marvelous plan to redeem the world. Will you become his partner?

Release Your Shame

Take a deep breath. Exhale the memories, thoughts, and distractions that run through your mind. Make your breathing slow and steady, and push all distractions away. Breathe in God's peace. Ask the Holy Spirit to take over. Let yourself feel his heartbeat inside of you.

Lift your eyes toward heaven or bow your head in prayer. Get on your knees or simply sit still. Now picture taking all your shame and handing it over to God. How does trusting God with your shame feel?

Now imagine him taking all the things you've done in the past, all those sins that bring you shame, and showing you how all your experiences make you the perfect choice to go into partnership with him to reach the world with the love of Jesus.

If you have struggled with addiction, what kind of impact could you have if you took that experience and reached out to those who are currently experiencing the pain of addiction? Let them see how the light of Jesus brought you out of that darkness.

If you have struggled with sexual sin, Jesus can redeem

you like he did the woman at the well. As he reveals himself to you, he empowers you to reveal him to others who are struggling in the same area.

Whatever is in your past is forgiven, and God will use it for his glory. Ask him to do that, and he will. You can experience the joy of seeing God use you to point people to him. What a turnabout!

Dear heavenly Father, I am so tired of shame keeping me up at night and waking me in the morning. My shame makes me run from you. I try to pray, but memories from my past—things I couldn't control and things I can't take back—flood me with shame. The shame clouds my mind and overwhelms my heart. Sometimes I feel as if I'm sleepwalking through life, self-sabotaging my best efforts and dreams. Help me experience the truth that can transform my shame and use it for your purposes. Thank you for loving me so much. I'm surrendering my shame to you. I'm choosing your truth, your love, your freedom. I want to be used by you for good because I know that you are good and that you love me. In the transforming name of Jesus I pray, amen.

JOURNAL PROMPT: As you reflect on the lives of Nicky Cruz, Chuck Colson, and the woman at the well, how can you see your story being used by God? Write down some ideas of people who might listen to you talk about Jesus because of what you've experienced.

PART 7

ANGER

Managing Your Anger

Reflect on God's Word

Proverb after proverb talks about the dangers of giving in to anger, to the extent that Proverbs 22:24 says, "Do not make friends with a hot-tempered person, do not associate with one easily angered."

Is uncontrolled anger weighing you down?

Anger is an emotional state of mind that can range from mild irritation to uncontrolled rage. Some people describe anger as a "secondary emotion." Unhealed hurts can lead to anger. So can unaddressed frustration and disappointment. For this reason, it is important to acknowledge what you are feeling so you can cast those cares on God.

It is normal to feel these emotions from time to time. But while we might *feel* these emotions, we need to remember that Colossians 3:8 gives us God's word on managing anger: "But now you must also rid yourselves of all such things as these: anger, rage, malice, slander, and filthy language from your lips."

It is not enough to put anger to the side. God's Word says to "rid yourselves." Think of it like cleaning your closet. When you get rid of all the things you don't need, not only can you find the things you *do* need, you also have space for better things.

This is what Philippians 4:8 suggests: "Finally, brothers and sisters, whatever is true, whatever is noble, whatever is right, whatever is pure, whatever is lovely, whatever is admirable—if anything is excellent or praiseworthy—think about such things."

If someone cuts you off in traffic, instead of lashing out in anger, turn on some music that brings your thoughts back to God. When your child causes you to feel anger boiling up inside, take a deep breath and focus on the last time they made you laugh.

Picture a pitcher full of soapy water. If the suds are your anger, continuing to pour in more soap will cause more and more bubbles to grow, but if instead you let pure, clear water flow into the pitcher, the suds will be pushed out until the pitcher is only full of that pure water.

God's Word is that pure, clear water. Consider memorizing Scripture so that the Holy Spirit can bring those passages to mind when anger wants to fill you up.

James 1:19–20 says, "My dear brothers and sisters, take note of this: Everyone should be quick to listen, slow to speak and slow to become angry, because human anger does not produce the righteousness that God desires."

God knows how anger affects you and the people around you. He doesn't want angry thoughts in your head, heart, body, or soul. Whether you need forgiveness or healing, God has it for you. Nothing is too hard for him. He does not judge you. He loves you. He is eager to help you manage your anger.

The hardest thing to do is to look in the mirror and ask God to examine your heart and mind. But once it's revealed, you can heal. God wants to free you from anger's grasp so you can live the life he created you for, one that is focused on him.

Release Your Anger

Start the process of releasing the anger that is controlling you by taking a deep breath and letting go of any tension in your body. Anger produces tension. As you relax your neck and shoulders, your back, your abdomen, and your legs, picture the anger being released from your body. Feel a quiet stillness come over you as you breathe deeply in and out.

Not only can God help you manage your anger, he can also help you understand why you are angry. Step away from your anger for a moment. Hold it in your hand, examine it, and ask God, "Where is my anger coming from?" Are you holding on to hurt from your past? Has an offense left you broken? Does the injustice in the world make your heart ache? Is your anger rooted in a conflict you are having with someone?

Take some time now to pray for those who have hurt or offended you. As you pray, reflect on how seeing others through Christ's eyes offers peace, even within difficult circumstances or relationships. When conflict or tension arises in you, lift your struggle to Jesus. Feel his Spirit flooding your heart with his love and kindness, tenderly cultivating within you a heart that resembles his heart.

ANGER

Maybe your anger is justified, is coming from an emotion or a hidden hurt, or is triggered by a circumstance, but
responding in anger, rage, and malice only make things
worse. Slander and filthy talk push you away from God, the
very one who wants to—and who *can*—help you.

Ask God to reveal areas in your life where anger is
hiding. It is hard to hear God's word when you are holding
on to anger, when the emotions that come with anger are
wrapped around your heart. Envision yourself letting go of
your anger and letting God take over. Remind yourself of
God's advice in Colossians 3:8 and put them all away, like
shutting them in an iron cage and locking the door. Anger,
rage, malice, slander, and filthy language, lock them all
away. And then give God the key so you aren't tempted to
let them out again.

Dear heavenly Father, I know when I act on my anger
it separates me from you. I feel it. That's the last thing
I want. I need your love, strength, guidance, and forgiveness in every area of my life. I give you my heart,
mind, body, and soul. Clean out the junk in my life and
replace it with all that is lovely and honorable and
pure so there is no room for anger. Help me identify what is truly making me angry. In your strength, I
don't have to be weighed down by my anger any longer. I can live in your love, and regardless of how I feel,
I can respond to everything and everyone in a way
that glorifies you. In the name of Jesus I pray, amen.

JOURNAL PROMPT: Will you let God take you "behind the scenes" of your anger? Write down three things that have made you angry lately, and then ask yourself why you were angry in those situations. For each answer, ask why again until you think you've reached the root. Pray over each item.

Keeping Anger from Making
a Home in Your Heart

Reflect on God's Word

Several years ago, a Georgia woman drove by the home she was selling just to say goodbye to it. Instead, she was shocked to find that someone else had moved in! Another family said they found the house for rent on a local website, signed electronic documents, wired money to someone, and moved in. And despite what the legal owner said, they weren't planning on leaving anytime soon.[1]

Maybe you feel that way about your anger. You don't want it to be there, but somehow it has taken up residence in your heart, and you are filled with chaos instead of peace.

Ecclesiastes 7:9 says, "Do not be quickly provoked in your spirit, for anger resides in the lap of fools."

That's a short verse filled with power. Some translations render the word *resides* as *lodges*. Picture what that means. Can you see anger making a home in your heart? It would love to take up permanent residence, set up a mailbox, and start redecorating.

When anger resides in your house, it leaves its mess wherever it goes. It leaves dishes in the sink, punches holes in the walls, and never takes out the trash. The person who lets anger sit within easy reach is called a fool. That couldn't be clearer, could it?

Why is letting anger take up residence in you foolish? Because it breaks your fellowship with God and with other people. But there is hope. If you have the Holy Spirit living in you, there will be no room for your anger. You can instead display the fruits of the Spirit: love, joy, peace, patience. All these and more displace anger and wrath.

What do you want your heart to look like?

Maybe you've seen the show *Extreme Makeover: Home Edition*. A group of workers comes in and totally remakes a home for a family in great need. Maybe they have someone who has special physical needs, or maybe they've just adopted several children who had lost their parents and they have no space. There have even been homes that have been ruined by water damage or pests. Whatever the reason, the home is not meeting the needs of the family, and they're not financially able to either get a new home or fix the one they have.

Perhaps you feel incapable of fixing your heart. Anger just seems to keep showing up at your door. It's time to let God do an extreme makeover on your heart so there is no place for anger to reside. You might let it in for a moment and ask it why it's there, but you don't let it put up its feet and make itself at home.

Letting the Holy Spirit fill up your heart looks like spending time with God in prayer, reading and meditating on his Word. It looks like surrounding yourself with other people who love God and want to live pure and Christ-centered lives. Let your heart be a home that attracts others instead of pushing them away.

Release Your Anger

If anger has been residing in your heart for a long time, it might take a lot of time to uproot it, but remember that you don't have to do this in your own strength. Spend some time meditating on God's Word and asking the Holy Spirit for help moment by moment, day by day. Ask him to bring to mind Scriptures that will fill your heart, pushing out those deep-seated feelings. Sometimes it's easy to forget to pray, to talk to God and allow his peace to fill you. Ask him to remind you of his presence and ownership of your heart.

Take a deep breath. Ask the Spirit of God to reveal any angry thoughts, desires, or actions within you. What recent incident sparked anger in you? What person recently got on your nerves? What effect did anger have on you or on your witness as a Christian this week?

Examine your heart. Take time to evaluate your feelings when anger shows up. Don't ignore it because it will subtly take over if you pretend it's not there. Make it a practice to look at your anger, ask it where it comes from, and then tell it that it's no longer welcome to stay.

Resisting anger can be a battle, but one that the Spirit of God is poised and ready to help you win! Don't let anger take up residence. Kick it to the curb. Gaining control in this area is a major step toward mental wellness.

Lord God, help me not to be angry in my heart. Resentful, deep-seated anger separates me from you. When I am quick-tempered, I know it exposes my foolishness for everyone to see. I don't want to be a fool. And I know anger only leads to evil. But it's hard. Anger shows up at my door sometimes, often when I least expect it. And so quickly. Please put someone in my life who has the courage to point out to me when I give an angry response. Give me greater understanding of my emotions so I can profit from self-control. I can't do this on my own. I need your strength, your grace, your mercy. I want my heart to be your home, filled with love, joy, peace, patience, kindness, goodness, gentleness, faithfulness, and self-control. It's in the name of Jesus that I pray, amen.

JOURNAL PROMPT: Write down some ways you can keep anger from taking up residence in your heart. What good things can you invite in instead?

Forget Pursuing Revenge

Reflect on God's Word

In the classic Alexandre Dumas story *The Count of Monte Cristo*, Edmond Dantès lives a seemingly perfect life, which causes three of his so-called friends to become wildly jealous of him. Because of their jealousy, they hatch a plot to have Edmond unjustly accused of treason and imprisoned. Edmond spends the next two decades of his life plotting revenge against his enemies. When he is finally able to escape from prison, he sets out to carry through his plans for revenge, throwing in some kind deeds along the way.[2]

Can you imagine spending more than half your life focused on getting revenge on those who have wronged you? Maybe you can, because you know how it feels for that desire and drive to weigh you down until you don't know how to get out from under it.

The desire to take revenge can be powerful, but it can also be so dangerous. It can cloud our judgment, penetrate our thoughts, and leave us bitter and miserable as we try to do something that God never intended for us to do.

Most often, revenge comes back to bite us, as psychotherapist Beverly Engel describes in an article from the *Washington Post*:

"When someone persists in revenge fantasies, over time they can develop anxiety and remorse, as well as feelings of shame," says California-based psychotherapist Beverly Engel, who treats clients who have been abused and often struggle with vengeful thoughts. These feelings can also take up important cognitive resources, depleting you of time and energy that could be better spent on healthier, more constructive ways of dealing with anger, such as learning to accept the injustice, putting yourself in the other person's shoes or acknowledging that you, too, may have hurt someone in similar ways.[3]

In Romans 12:17–21, the apostle Paul cautions,

Do not repay anyone evil for evil. Be careful to do what is right in the eyes of everyone. If it is possible, as far as it depends on you, live at peace with everyone. Do not take revenge, my dear friends, but leave room for God's wrath, for it is written: "It is mine to avenge; I will repay," says the Lord. On the contrary:

"If your enemy is hungry, feed him;
    if he is thirsty, give him something to
        drink.

In doing this, you will heap burning coals on
his head."

Do not be overcome by evil, but overcome evil
with good.

Heap burning coals on their head? That sounds like a form of revenge, doesn't it? But that verse is from Proverbs 25:21–22. The entire proverb is a collection of sayings that deal with interactions between people. Don't sing songs to a person in mourning (v. 20), hearing good news is like drinking cool water when you're weary (v. 25), relying on someone who is unfaithful is like walking with a lame leg or eating with a broken tooth (v. 19). In a society that depended on fire for cooking and keeping warm, burning coals were a gift of sustenance if one's fire had gone out. And God says to not just give them one to get it going again, but to heap burning coals on them. Go above and beyond in kindness.[4]

Our desire for vengeance comes from our desire to see justice done. We forget so easily that justice has *already been done*. The person who hurt us will pay for what he or she did, either by receiving forgiveness from God and allowing Christ to take the penalty for their sin, or by spending eternity separated from God because of their sin. Either way, justice will prevail. And when we think of justice this way, our hearts can soften toward the person who hurt us.

If you wrestle with wanting to have vengeance, remember that God has the situation under control. If you begin to feel destructive anger burning inside of you, allow Christ's healing, life-giving water to quench those flames as you focus instead on his forgiveness, his grace, and his mercy. Remember, God loved you long before you saw your need for him (Romans 5:8), and he loves the person who wronged you just as much.

Release Your Anger

Take a long, deep, slow breath. Hold it for a moment, and then release it very slowly. Do that again. Feel the release through the power of the Holy Spirit as you continue to breathe deeply and slowly. With each exhale, release your pain and anger to God. With each inhale, feel his healing love flow in.

How would your life change if the desire for revenge lost its grip on you?

Rather than pursuing vengeance, give that care to God and ask him to soften and expand your heart with love for others. God's love can bring healing and soften that grip.

Imagine a desert. For each painful feeling you carry inside of you because of others—mistrust, fear, anger, hate—picture a crack splitting the dry ground into deep, sharp crevices. Now, picture a gentle rain falling on the dry land, gradually softening the hard ground until the crevices fill and merge back into the earth. Feel a gentle breeze and warm sunlight as plants begin to emerge from the now-tender earth. As this image fades from your mind, pay attention to how your heart feels. How do you relate to the image of the barren desert? How do you relate to the field bursting with life?

Now picture your desire for revenge smoldering inside you. Feel the burning pain of it. And then picture your heart healing as Christ's Spirit quenches those flames with life-giving, healing water. Then rest in the comfort of his arms. Breathe in deeply once more, reflecting on how the just God you serve knows your pain and wants to heal you and use you in the lives of those around you.

Lord, it's hard sometimes not to let anger consume me, especially when people hurt others, including me. I know you've forgiven me, but sometimes I'm so angry at others I'd prefer revenge to seeing them come to know your forgiving love. Forgive me for this. Heal and soften my heart. Thank you that new life is possible through you, that deserts can become pools of water. Thank you that no one can force fear, anger, or hate to live on in me. Each day, help me know more deeply that your love is stronger than anything anyone can do to me. Show me what it means to walk in true love and freedom. I long for your love, justice, and beauty to fill this earth. Until that day, help me find peace in your love. In Jesus' name, amen.

JOURNAL PROMPT: How have you seen your desire for revenge affect your relationships? What effect has it had on your health? Journal about how your heart can find the healing it needs to be free from this desire for revenge.

Tame Your Tongue

Reflect on God's Word

There have been a few cases in recent years when a news anchor thought they were off mic and proceeded to say something that ended up being broadcast, causing them great embarrassment, and in some cases to lose their jobs. Inappropriate jokes, bad language, and mean-spirited comments all come from a tongue that has not been tamed by the Holy Spirit. And like trying to get toothpaste back into a tube once it has been squeezed out, words, especially on the internet, live on forever.

Have you fallen victim to your own tongue? Maybe outbursts of anger have gotten you in trouble, as you say exactly what's on your mind with no filter. Anger often expresses itself in our words, and we say things we later wish we could take back. Are your seemingly unstoppable words causing chaos in your life?

James thought this issue was so important that he dedicated several paragraphs to talking about it in his letter to the dispersed Jews:

When we put bits into the mouths of horses to make them obey us, we can turn the whole animal. Or take ships as an example. Although they are so large and are driven by strong winds, they are steered by a very small rudder wherever the pilot wants to go. Likewise, the tongue is a small part of the body, but it makes great boasts. Consider what a great forest is set on fire by a small spark. The tongue also is a fire, a world of evil among the parts of the body. It corrupts the whole body, sets the whole course of one's life on fire, and is itself set on fire by hell.

All kinds of animals, birds, reptiles and sea creatures are being tamed and have been tamed by mankind, but no human being can tame the tongue. It is a restless evil, full of deadly poison.

With the tongue we praise our Lord and Father, and with it we curse human beings, who have been made in God's likeness. Out of the same mouth come praise and cursing. My brothers and sisters, this should not be. Can both fresh water and salt water flow from the same spring? My brothers and sisters, can a fig tree bear olives, or a grapevine bear figs? Neither can a salt spring produce fresh water. (James 3:3–12)

God knows you will get angry. What he wants is for you to be in control of that anger, not for it to be in control of you. When emotions are heightened, it is easy to go back to old habits and say and do things you will regret—or at least not be proud of.

This does not have to be your story.

God knows you will be tempted to react negatively when you are angry. But you do not have to give in to the temptation. God's word, wisdom, and power are in you. You can learn to tame your tongue. You don't have to lash out.

When you find yourself wanting to say something in anger, a good first step is to check your heart. Luke 6:45 records Jesus as saying, "A good man brings good things out of the good stored up in his heart, and an evil man brings evil things out of the evil stored up in his heart. For the mouth speaks what the heart is full of." What is your heart full of? When anger boils up, step back instead of stepping into a potential mess. Ask the Holy Spirit to show you the root of that anger.

Another good practice is to listen more and speak less. This can give you the opportunity to hear what another person has to say instead of just reacting to the situation. Proverbs 17:27 says, "The one who has knowledge uses words with restraint, and whoever has understanding is even-tempered." Practice restraint when you are interacting with others. Maybe you need to count to ten and take several deep breaths to cool down so you don't say something in anger. Seek to understand instead of lashing out.

Finally, make it a point to build people up instead of tearing them down. Ephesians 4:29 says, "Do not let any unwholesome talk come out of your mouths, but only what is helpful for building others up according to their needs, that it may benefit those who listen." Are your words beneficial, or are they cutting? Do you come away from your interactions with others feeling good about them and yourself, or did you let your anger take over?

Taming your tongue is not only important for building up the body of Christ, it's also important for those who do not follow Jesus to see that you have self-control and that you live out your faith in the words you say. James again addressed this issue in his letter.

> Do not merely listen to the word, and so deceive your-selves. Do what it says. Anyone who listens to the word but does not do what it says is like someone who looks at his face in a mirror and, after looking at himself, goes away and immediately forgets what he looks like. But whoever looks intently into the perfect law that gives freedom, and continues in it—not forgetting what they have heard, but doing it—they will be blessed in what they do.
>
> Those who consider themselves religious and yet do not keep a tight rein on their tongues deceive themselves, and their religion is worthless. (James 1:22–26)

Let your talk reflect your walk. If you have the Holy Spirit living inside you, you have all the power you need to keep your tongue—and your anger—under control.

Release Your Anger

Take a deep breath. If you have found your tongue being controlled by anger, take steps to let the Holy Spirit control it instead. Lift your hands toward heaven and ask the Holy Spirit to take over. Thank God out loud for helping you exercise self-control in the midst of your anger. Thank him for the peace he offers, even in your anger.

Picture your words like sparks drifting up from a campfire. As each one leaves your mouth, it falls at the feet of the person you're interacting with. Are those sparks, those words coming out of your mouth, going to provide warmth to the one who receives it, or will it start a conflagration that destroys?

You are frustrated with your child because they are not moving as quickly as you need them to when you're trying to leave the house for school. How do you speak to them? Will they go to school with a smile on their face because you restrained from speaking in anger but instead focused on being kind, or will they carry a wound in their spirit from the harsh words you said?

If you are listening to someone speak in favor of something you strongly disagree with in a public place, do you speak with anger against them, using inappropriate language to denigrate them, or do you let the Holy Spirit build gentleness in you and ask questions to help you better understand their story?

In both of these circumstances, prayer is vital. Connecting your heart with God's heart will help you see people as he sees them: as image bearers of God who deserve honor and grace.

Dear God, I am overwhelmed by your love. Thank you for sharing your wisdom with me. Thank you for telling me that my tongue does not have to be controlled by my anger. Help me tame my tongue. I know you are with me, filling me with your Spirit. And I know you love me. Let me feel your love. Pour your love over the areas in my life that need it the most. Where there is anger, replace it with your peace. Revive any area where bitterness has made a home. Show me why it is hard sometimes to control my anger. Help me be more like you. In Jesus' name I pray, amen.

JOURNAL PROMPT: What practical steps can you take to tame your tongue? Write down three things. Carry them with you. Remember, with God's strength, you can do this.

The Power of Forgiveness

Reflect on God's Word

When one of the Pharisees invited Jesus to have dinner with him, he went to the Pharisee's house and reclined at the table. A woman in that town who lived a sinful life learned that Jesus was eating at the Pharisee's house, so she came there with an alabaster jar of perfume. As she stood behind him at his feet weeping, she began to wet his feet with her tears. Then she wiped them with her hair, kissed them and poured perfume on them.

When the Pharisee who had invited him saw this, he said to himself, "If this man were a prophet, he would know who is touching him and what kind of woman she is—that she is a sinner."

Jesus answered him, "Simon, I have something to tell you."

"Tell me, teacher," he said.

"Two people owed money to a certain money-lender. One owed him five hundred denarii, and the other fifty. Neither of them had the money to pay him back, so he forgave the debts of both. Now which of them will love him more?"

Simon replied, "I suppose the one who had the bigger debt forgiven."

"You have judged correctly," Jesus said.

Then he turned toward the woman and said to Simon, "Do you see this woman? I came into your house. You did not give me any water for my feet, but she wet my feet with her tears and wiped them with her hair. You did not give me a kiss, but this woman, from the time I entered, has not stopped kissing my feet. You did not put oil on my head, but she has poured perfume on my feet. Therefore, I tell you, her many sins have been forgiven—as her great love has shown. But whoever has been forgiven little loves little." (Luke 7:36–47)

Picture that story. A humble woman, knowing she was a sinner, coming in uninvited to a dinner. She approaches Jesus and shows him respect and love. For that, her sins were forgiven. Imagine the shame she felt. Imagine the stares. How do you think she felt?

Imagine being her and feeling the acceptance and love of Christ. No condemnation. Imagine offering that same freedom to those who have hurt you. What a transformation that could make in your heart! Instead of holding on to anger, feeling the heavy weight of it every time you move, you can be at peace.

You might have heard it said that not forgiving someone is like drinking poison and hoping the other person dies. Or sitting in a locked cell with the key to freedom in your own hands. But sometimes in our anger, we want to sit in that cell. The comic strip *Rose Is Rose* often shows Rose, the main character, sitting at the bottom of a deep well, arms crossed, face glowering, as she holds on to resentment from a wound she received from her husband. Even as her husband calls her from above, telling her he's sorry and that he loves her, she stays in her deep well.

Does your anger and resentment keep you shackled? Holding on to hurts and not forgiving can take an enormous physical toll.

An article titled "Forgiveness: Your Health Depends on It" from Johns Hopkins Medicine states, "'There is an enormous physical burden to being hurt and disappointed,' says Karen Swartz, M.D., director of the Mood Disorders Adult Consultation Clinic at The Johns Hopkins Hospital. Chronic anger puts you into a fight-or-flight mode, which results in numerous changes in heart rate, blood pressure and immune response. Those changes, then, increase the risk of depression, heart disease and diabetes, among other conditions. Forgiveness, however, calms stress levels, leading to improved health."[5]

Maybe you have a hard time forgiving *yourself*. An article titled "Forgiving Yourself" on AllAboutGOD.com says, "Proverbs 16:25 says, 'There is a way that seems right to a man, but its end is the way of death.' The energy it takes to harbor anger, hatred, and resentment towards yourself is exhaustive. Every bit of energy we give to negative activities and dwelling on regrets, robs us of the energy we need to become the person God wants us to be."[6]

You are only healed from your guilt by the wounds of Jesus (1 Peter 2:24). Allow knowing how much he paid for you to build up love inside you like an unending treasure. This love can make it possible for you to handle the cost of forgiving others. It has the power to make you a part of God's healing process and plan to reconcile all things to him (2 Corinthians 5:18–21).

Find a moment today to offer forgiveness to someone who crosses you. It may be undeserved, but pardon them. Offer them grace—the same grace God offers you through Christ.

Release Your Anger

Stop for a moment to release the tension that might have started building in your body. Take a deep breath and hold it for just a moment before releasing it. Extending forgiveness is not easy or natural, but it's necessary.

Start by forgiving yourself for any guilt you feel. Jesus has forgiven you. Allow him to bring healing and fill you with his love. Bring your wounds caused by others to him. Jesus has forgiven them, too. Ask for his Spirit to help you do the same.

Take a few more deep, cleansing breaths. Forgiving breaths. See Jesus on the cross, bearing your sins, extending forgiveness, even to those who hung him there (Luke 23:34). Open your hands to symbolize your willingness to let go of your hurts and allow God to heal your wounds.

Now picture a heavy chain with many links shackling you to the bottom of a deep well. As you think about each hurt you're holding on to, picture a link in that chain. Now touch one link. Think about the hurt that link represents. As you touch it in your mind, extend forgiveness to the person who hurt you. See the link break as you do it. Do that for each link: touch it, forgive, and see it break. Continue until all the links are broken and your chain falls off.

It's important to remember that forgiveness of someone who deeply hurt you does not necessarily mean that there will be restoration of the relationship. If you suffered abuse, you need to be safe. But extending forgiveness is vital for your soul to live free.

Each time you feel anger building in you, stop and look at your heart. Are you holding on to a hurt or something from your past? Picture that chain. Break the link with forgiveness and feel the peace that comes with forgiveness.

By forgiving others—and yourself—you free yourself to be all God wants you to be. The roots of your anger can be pulled up, never to grow strong again.

Dear God, as I look for the courage to forgive others, I need look no further than the courage of your Son, who died so I might be forgiven. Thank you for your forgiveness of my sins. Help me remember to extend the same forgiveness to others. Help me remove the chains that bind me. In Jesus' name, amen.

JOURNAL PROMPT: Journal your thoughts on being forgiven for your most secret sin. How can you offer that same freedom to someone who has hurt you?

PART 8

IDENTITY

Hear the Applause of God

Reflect on God's Word

Ludwig van Beethoven stood facing the orchestra as the last notes of his Symphony no. 9 faded away. After it was over, he continued to face the musicians, perhaps wondering where he had gone wrong. Why was there no applause from the audience?

Finally, a singer approached one of the greatest composers of all time, turned him around, and let him see the wild, thundering applause raining down on him from the crowd.

You see, by the time his Symphony no. 9 in D Minor, op. 125, also known as the Choral Symphony, was premiered in 1824, Beethoven was profoundly deaf. He couldn't hear the applause of the people.[1]

Are you sometimes deaf to the applause of God? Sometimes we can be so focused on winning the approval of others that we forget how very much God approves of us.

In Galatians 1:10, the apostle Paul addresses this very issue: "Am I now trying to win the approval of human beings, or of God? Or am I trying to please people? If I were still trying to please people, I would not be a servant of Christ."

Paul had much to recommend about himself: "If someone else thinks they have reasons to put confidence in the flesh, I have more: circumcised on the eighth day, of the people of Israel, of the tribe of Benjamin, a Hebrew of Hebrews; in regard to the law, a Pharisee; as for zeal, persecuting the church; as for righteousness based on the law, faultless" (Philippians 3:4–6).

But you know what Paul says next? "But whatever were gains to me I now consider loss for the sake of Christ" (Philippians 3:7).

What a burden it is to try to please everyone. Paul told the Corinthians that he became all things to all people so he might save some (1 Corinthians 9:22), but his goal was not to make people like him; it was to proclaim the gospel in a way people could hear. When your goal is to be liked, it may feel good to please others, but when you fail to do so the next time, it can send you spiraling down.

Paul wrote to the Thessalonians about this issue of pleasing people as well. "We speak as those approved by God to be entrusted with the gospel. We are not trying to please people but God, who tests our hearts. You know we never used flattery, nor did we put on a mask to cover up greed—God is our witness. We were not looking for praise from people, not from you or anyone else, even though as apostles of Christ we could have asserted our authority" (1 Thessalonians 2:4–6).

So how do you listen to the approval you already have from God (1 Thessalonians 2:4)? First Corinthians 4:5 says, "Therefore judge nothing before the appointed time; wait until the Lord comes. He will bring to light what is hidden in darkness and will expose the motives of the heart. At that time each will receive their praise from God."

About this verse, missionary and Bible teacher Rick Renner wrote, "Paul used the word *epainos* to evoke a very strong image. By using this word, he let us know that a day is coming when we will give account for our lives. On that day, if we have lived right before God and the motives behind our service were pure, we will receive praise from the Lord Himself. It will be as if He rises to His feet to give *a round of applause* and *a standing ovation*! In fact, Paul's imagery is so strong that the verse could be loosely interpreted, *"And at that time every man will have the applause of God."*[2]

Picture that moment. You stand before the throne of God and he looks over your life, all you've done, your motivations for doing them, your heart. And then he stands to his feet and begins to applaud you. You hear the words "Well done, good and faithful servant" (Matthew 25:21).

All you ever heard from the people in your life before this moment pales in comparison. All those times when you did something you really didn't want to do, but you wanted the approval of the person asking? Forgotten. Those times when you said something you didn't really feel because you knew the person listening wanted to hear it? Gone.

Waking up in the morning wanting to be liked, accepted, and admired can be a fearsome burden, causing you to question everything you do and everything that's true about you. But you are fearfully and wonderfully made (Psalm 139:14);

you sparkle like jewels (Zechariah 9:16); you are his treas-
ured possession (Malachi 3:17).

Be still and listen to the applause of your heavenly Father.
When you focus on him and live to please him, you will find
greater peace.

Release Who You Thought You Were

God invites you to rest peacefully in the knowledge
that he has called you and made you worthy. Take a deep
breath. Don't look anywhere else but to him for your val-
idation. Turn the eyes of your heart toward Jesus and his
great love for you.

Breathe in: I am God's child.

Breathe out: I am fearfully and wonderfully made.

Let your breathing grow deeper and slower as you hold
those words close.

I am God's child.

I am fearfully and wonderfully made.

Think about the way you feel when someone praises
you. Those words of encouragement are a gift from God
and should be enjoyed as such. But if you rely on words of
praise from others to feel valuable and appreciated, you are
falling into a trap. Ask God to show you ways to break free
of the need to be praised.

If you worried less about what other people thought of
you, how would that change the way you approach the work
God has given you to do? If he calls you to lead a Bible study
and somebody thinks you should work in the nursery instead,

do you succumb to their wishes, or continue doing what God asked you to do?

Maybe you want to be a part of a group at work or at school, but they are participating in activities you have decided you don't want to participate in. Do you bow to the pressure to join in just so they will like you, or do you stick to your convictions and maybe experience rejection?

Call to mind some areas of your life where you have been seeking people's approval. Offer those areas to God. It's human nature to want to be accepted, but when you strive to please others, forgetting how much you are accepted by God, you live in fear of rejection instead of finding your peace in Christ.

When you don't hear applause from others, close your eyes and hear the applause of God. Even when you are doing nothing but resting, God approves of *you*. Let that truth sink deeply into your soul. Draw near to him in prayer, and he will show you how he wants you to live.

God, you made me and called me a good creation. And while I was still a sinner, you sent your Son, Jesus, to free me from my sin and reconcile me to you. You've called me your child and given me every spiritual blessing. When I'm feeling insecure and look to others for approval, help me seek comfort in these truths. It's so easy for me to want the applause of people, but when I am commended by people, it might feel good in the moment, but it never seems to last. I'm just one decision away from doing something they disapprove of. It's a roller coaster! Teach me to look to you for my sense of worth and to embrace the truth that I am approved by you. It's in the name of Jesus that I pray, amen.

JOURNAL PROMPT: Write down the times when you typically find yourself most tempted to seek the approval of others. What do you think God would have you do in these situations?

Live as an Overcomer

Reflect on God's Word

What does it mean to be an overcomer?

Brazilian Paralympian swimmer Daniel Dias entered this world in 1989 with only one fully formed limb, his left leg. His arms and his right leg were stunted, leaving him with just one finger on his left hand. He was laughed at by the other children in school. He was called "cripple."

He says, "When I started school I was the different one, for having the disability. So the children would look, and I would feel embarrassed. I was called names—moments that really hurt—I would arrive home crying many times, and it wasn't anything easy. It was then that God gave a lot of wisdom to my parents. My mom and my dad would talk a lot with me, and I made a choice in my life: I chose to be happy. And this choice changed my life."[3]

By the time he turned twenty-six, Daniel had won twenty-two medals in swimming and held ten world records for para-athletics.

He knew God had created him for a reason.

So what does it mean to be an overcomer? Here's what it doesn't mean: It doesn't mean you have to perform perfectly, work harder, or be better. It doesn't mean you have to be successful or look like you have everything together. You don't have to conquer your fears or climb the highest mountain.

To be an overcomer, you need to abide in Christ because *he* has overcome the world.

Listen to what Jesus said to his disciples the day before his death, as recorded in John 16:33: "I have told you these things, so that in me you may have peace. In this world you will have trouble. But take heart! I have overcome the world."

In this verse, Jesus promises that despite all the failures and trials and difficulties you will face, you can have confidence that the victory over whatever it is you are facing is already yours.

Maybe you struggle with addiction. It has a hold on you that you can't seem to break. You think it will have power over you forever. Jesus invites you to trust him to overcome your addiction. Sometimes the intervention of professionals is needed if your addiction is chemical, but 1 Corinthians 15:56–57 says, "The sting of death is sin, and the power of sin is the law. But thanks be to God! He gives us the victory through our Lord Jesus Christ."

And just before that, in 1 Corinthians 10:13, Paul says, "No temptation has overtaken you except what is common to mankind. And God is faithful; he will not let you be tempted beyond what you can bear. But when you are tempted, he will also provide a way out so that you can endure it."

So being an overcomer looks like taking God at his word.

If you have the Holy Spirit living within you, you have the power to resist the temptation to give in to sin.

Maybe you have faced a trial you think will never end. Maybe it's the serious illness of a loved one, or even yourself. Chronic illness and pain take a huge toll. Jesus invites you to rest in the truth of Romans 8:28: "And we know that in all things God works for the good of those who love him, who have been called according to his purpose."

So being an overcomer looks like trusting that God has not abandoned you, and his plan for you is good because he is good (Psalm 100:5).

Maybe, like Daniel Dias, you were born with disabilities, or you sustained life-altering injuries in an accident, like Joni Eareckson Tada, who became paralyzed from the shoulders down when she fractured her spine. Jesus invites you to trust him as your creator and sustainer. First Samuel 16:7 says, "People look at the outward appearance, but the LORD looks at the heart." Whatever your disability, you are more than able.

Ephesians 3:20–21 says, "Now to him who is able to do immeasurably more than all we ask or imagine, according to his power that is at work within us, to him be glory in the church and in Christ Jesus throughout all generations, for ever and ever! Amen."

So being an overcomer looks like leaning into the power of God to do whatever he wants through you. No comparisons, no excuses, nothing holding you back from being all he created you to be.

God does not promise you a life free of difficulties. In fact, Jesus promises that on earth you will have trials and sorrows. But he also promises to be with you in those sorrows, and he invites you to find courage and comfort in his victory moment by moment, day by day.

Release Who You Thought You Were

Jesus wants to bring peace to your heart as you hear his truth. Take a few moments now and ask him to speak straight to you, where you are, and to give you his peace.

Notice your breath moving in and out. Let go of other thoughts, worries, or distractions, and just attend to your breath. Let it grow deeper and slower. Inhale and feel the air moving into your chest and belly, and then exhale slowly, pushing it out. Let your muscles relax. Soften your neck and shoulders. Let them fall. Rest here, just attending to your breath.

Think about someone you know who has trusted in God through difficult circumstances. What did it look like for that person to take God at his word, to trust him, to lean into his power despite going through all kinds of trials?

Name some of the circumstances you would like to overcome. Picture each one as a book. Close each book and put it in a backpack. Now hand that backpack over to Jesus and say, "I trust you with these—all of them—even if things don't work out the way I want them to."

Imagine Jesus now taking your bag and giving you a little white bird. It perches on your shoulder and sings comfort and truth to you. That's the Holy Spirit speaking to your heart. Hear Jesus say to you, "I am with you! I will never leave your side."

Whether you're able to trust Jesus completely with your difficulties, or whether you're already trying to take that backpack back—the Father loves you, always has and always will.

Breathe in the peace Jesus offers. You don't need to work harder or strive to be better to find peace or overcome the trials in your life. All you need to do is abide in Jesus. Immerse yourself in the Scriptures. Spend intentional time in prayer. Surround yourself with like-minded Christians. Jesus is your peace, your worth, your life. In him and with his strength, you have overcome the world.

God, sometimes I feel as if it is all I can do to get out of bed and make it through another day. Overcoming just sounds overwhelming! Thank you for this reminder that Jesus has overcome the world, and I don't have to. Help me place my trust in Jesus and abide in him as I seek to live into the identity you've given me. Thank you for sending Jesus to take on human flesh and to conquer sin and death. Thank you for making a way for me to be united with him. Help me learn to put my confidence in Jesus and not in myself—to lighten my load by abiding in him instead of struggling on my own to find victory. It's in his strong name I pray, amen.

JOURNAL PROMPT: Think about those circumstances you named above. How have you been trying to overcome them on your own? How would it look to focus on abiding in Christ and letting him strengthen you into an overcomer?

Rejoice in Your Freedom

Reflect on God's Word

Listen to the story of the woman caught in adultery from John 8:2–11:

At dawn [Jesus] appeared again in the temple courts, where all the people gathered around him, and he sat down to teach them. The teachers of the law and the Pharisees brought in a woman caught in adultery. They made her stand before the group and said to Jesus, "Teacher, this woman was caught in the act of adultery. In the Law Moses commanded us to stone such women. Now what do you say?" They were using this question as a trap, in order to have a basis for accusing him.

But Jesus bent down and started to write on the ground with his finger. When they kept on questioning him, he straightened up and said to them, "Let any one of you who is without sin be the first to throw a stone at her." Again he stooped down and wrote on the ground.

At this, those who heard began to go away one at a time, the older ones first, until only Jesus was left, with the woman still standing there. Jesus straightened up and

asked her, "Woman, where are they? Has no one condemned you?"

"No one, sir," she said.

"Then neither do I condemn you," Jesus declared.
"Go now and leave your life of sin."

This woman should have felt condemned because she
knew she had sinned. She was caught in the very act, dragged
before Jesus by her accusers, and labeled as an adulteress.
But Jesus, knowing the hearts of everyone who stood there,
called them all out: "Let any one of you who is without sin
be the first to throw a stone at her."

And then those words that would echo in her mind for
the rest of her life: "Neither do I condemn you."

Everyone experiences feelings of inferiority, condemnation, and hopelessness from time to time, but if we dwell in
those feelings, we cannot enjoy the life God has called us to
live because we live under a cloud of guilt. This burden can
turn into depression, shame, and fear.

But 2 Corinthians 3:17–18 says, "Now the Lord is the
Spirit, and where the Spirit of the Lord is, there is free-
dom. And we all, who with unveiled faces contemplate the
Lord's glory, are being transformed into his image with ever-
increasing glory, which comes from the Lord, who is the
Spirit."

Day by day you are being transformed into the image of
Christ through the power of the Holy Spirit, and where the
Spirit of the Lord is, as Paul said, there is freedom. Ephesians

3:12 reminds us, "In him and through faith in him we may approach God with freedom and confidence."

When was the last time you approached God with confidence? If you are living under a veil of condemnation, you probably haven't wanted to approach God at all. But Jesus paid the penalty for all your sins. You can boldly approach his throne, free from guilt.

Hebrews 4:15–16 says, "For we do not have a high priest who is unable to empathize with our weaknesses, but we have one who has been tempted in every way, just as we are—yet he did not sin. Let us then approach God's throne of grace with confidence, so that we may receive mercy and find grace to help us in our time of need."

God is so merciful. He does not want you to cower in condemnation when he has set you free. That is a burden you are not intended to bear. Jesus already bore it on the cross.

Imagine again that woman caught in adultery. Jesus says he doesn't condemn her, and in that moment she feels completely free. Forgiven. She leaves that place rejoicing. And then she comes across her neighbor as she makes her way home. As her smiling eyes encounter her neighbor's, she reads condemnation. Her neighbor knows who she is, what she has done.

She wilts inside again at the reminder, lowering her head, hiding her face, slowing her pace. And then she feels a presence by her side. It's Jesus, and he is again saying to her, "Neither do I condemn you." She breathes in deeply, straightens her shoulders, smiles at her neighbor, and keeps walking.

She feels good for another few minutes, and then she encounters the man with whom she sinned. He laughs at her. The smile fades from her eyes again. Her steps slow again, her head bows, her heart is heavy.

Again she feels Jesus right by her side and hears his precious, life-giving words: "Neither do I condemn you."

Jesus breathes life into our shattered souls. He is the living water for our wilting spirits. Those five words have the power to set us free: Neither do I condemn you. Accept them. Embrace them. Rejoice in your freedom.

Release Who You Thought You Were

Take time now to slow your thoughts as you let the wonderful, freeing truth of God's love pour over you. Put aside distractions and breathe in the Holy Spirit's love and wisdom. Ask God to calm your heart and sharpen your mind so you can hear his still, small voice instead of the clamor of all that weighs on you.

If you have belonged to Christ for a while, reflect on the ways his life-giving Spirit has changed you. Using that as encouragement, ask him to help you see yourself today as he sees you (remember, there is no condemnation!).

Then take a moment to kneel mentally before God. Or physically do so, if it will help you. Picture him nearer to you than your own breath. Imagine his hand on your head, his arm holding you close. Let the reality of God's nearness and his perfect, unchanging love fill you with hope and belief.

See the mistakes you've made in the past like red ink on

a piece of paper, each one a separate slip. Maybe your pile of paper is so high it's overwhelming. Maybe there are just a few things that you feel truly guilty for. Whatever the case, watch as Jesus takes each one and, from the nail mark in his hand, lets his blood drip. As the red of his blood covers the red of those condemning words, they disappear completely. For each slip of paper, Jesus does the same thing as he says, "Neither do I condemn you."

> Dear heavenly Father, I am astounded at the truth of this message. You don't see my failings when you look at me; instead, you see me made perfect by the sinless Christ. That means there really is no condemnation for me because I am in you. You created me to be whole and holy. You want me to live abundantly and joyously, which is impossible if I am stuck on my own failures. Instead, I need to focus on your great love and power. Help me do that, Lord! I want to be set free from the way I condemn myself. In the power of your name I pray, amen.

JOURNAL PROMPT: Write down some of those things for which you have been condemning yourself. Now take a red pen and write these words: Neither Do I Condemn You.

Believe the Truth about
Who You Are

Reflect on God's Word

Where do you normally turn to boost your self-worth? Social media? Your friends who tell you what you want to hear? Do you go shopping or watch videos of the failings of others to make yourself feel better? Or do you follow the wisdom of Scripture, which says you are created in the image of God—loved and chosen by him for a purpose?

First Peter 2:9 says, "But you are a chosen people, a royal priesthood, a holy nation, God's special possession, that you may declare the praises of him who called you out of darkness into his wonderful light."

You have worth because of who you are in Christ: a member of a royal priesthood. Satan, though, wants you to doubt God. He wants you to live a life of guilt and regret, not one full of joy and peace.

In John 8:44, Jesus said to the Pharisees, "You belong to your father, the devil, and you want to carry out your father's desires. He was a murderer from the beginning, not holding to the truth, for there is no truth in him. When he lies, he speaks his native language, for he is a liar and the father of lies."

Think about that: Satan cannot tell the truth! Satan isn't simply a liar. He is the father of lies! Satan hates the truth. He doesn't want you to believe it when God says you are royal and holy. But you are both.

How should the truth about who you are impact how you live? Think about how Moses, King David, and the apostle Paul—all pillars of the faith—were affected when they listened to how God viewed them.

Moses once murdered someone. It would have been easy for him to believe that "murderer" would always be his identity. But he chose, instead, to listen to the truth, to believe that God was going to use him in a mighty way to free the Israelites from slavery in Egypt.

King David could have listened to Satan's lies. He could have believed that he was and always would be an adulterer and someone who plotted the death of an innocent man. But he chose, instead, to accept the truth spoken to him by the prophet Nathan (see 2 Samuel 12), to repent, and to humble himself before God. And God did mighty things through him to help save the nation of Israel from its enemies and ultimately to bring the Messiah through David's line.

The apostle Paul—as Saul—persecuted Jesus' followers. He could have listened to the lies that said he was good enough on his own. He certainly had the credentials. But, instead, he opened his heart to an encounter with the risen Christ. And God used him to spread the gospel around the world.

Clearly, God chooses sinful, flawed people to accomplish

his work—people convicted of sin by the Holy Spirit and then guided to God-honoring actions.

Your worth isn't determined by what you or others think. And it's definitely not determined by what Satan thinks. It's determined by the way God sees you: as someone he loves and wants to use for his purposes.

Release Who You Thought You Were

As you meditate on God's marvelous truth, take a deep, relaxing breath.

You are the temple of God (1 Corinthians 3:16–17).

You are a royal priesthood (1 Peter 2:9).

You are no longer a slave but an heir (Galatians 4:7).

You are a new creation (2 Corinthians 5:17).

You are his handiwork, created for good works (Ephesians 2:10).

Whisper to God, "Thank you for loving me and choosing me for a purpose."

As you continue meditating on God's Word, push away your self-doubt and anxiety.

Slow down and rest in God's peaceful presence. Open your palms heavenward, inviting God to surround you. Take another deep breath and imagine yourself inhaling his grace and mercy. Breathe out, as if you're casting your troubles on him. He's a big God. He can take care of them!

Take another deep, relaxing breath. Now breathe out. Think about when you are most likely to believe Satan's lies about who you are. Maybe it's when you're around certain friends. Maybe it's when you're alone. Ask God to help you confront Satan's lies with God's truth.

You are loved. You are forgiven. You are valuable. Don't believe the father of lies. Today, trust in the glorious God who saves.

Father, thank you for your love. Thank you for your peace, your mercy, your grace. I confess that, too often, I listen to the lies of Satan. Draw me closer to you. Help me see myself the way you see me: forgiven and holy. Fill me with joy. Encourage me. Give me power to defeat doubt. Thank you for saving me and loving me. Forgive me for the moments I listen to the lies of Satan instead of your perfect truth. You are a God who cannot lie, so I know that what you say about me is true. I'm grateful. Help me see myself the way you see me—as blessed, unique, and chosen. It's in Christ's name that I pray, amen.

JOURNAL PROMPT: How does knowing how God worked in the lives of Moses, King David, and the apostle Paul give you courage to accept God's truth (not Satan's lies) about who you are? What do you know is true about you from Scripture?

See Yourself as a Child of God

Reflect on God's Word

Kids whose parents show them love continually might not return the favor. They can disregard their parents' advice or lie to hide things from them. Some even shut out their parents altogether because of past disagreements and grudges. Other children receive love from their parents and learn how to show love themselves.

We can go either way as children of God.

John 1:12 tells us, "Yet to all who did receive him, to those who believed in his name, he gave the right to become children of God."

By God's grace, you have become a child of God. You have been adopted into his family. Being God's child is your highest calling. It gives you your purpose. Everything you do represents your heavenly Father. But just as some children may struggle with trusting their earthly parents, many people hold back from fully living as God's children.

Try saying out loud, "I am a child of God." Remind yourself that your Father in heaven has adopted you forever. The Holy Spirit lives in you to make you into his child.

Galatians 3:26 says: "So in Christ Jesus you are all

children of God through faith." We have the full rights and privileges of the heirs of God.

So what are those rights and privileges?

You have the privilege of being a peacemaker. In Matthew 5:9 Jesus said, "Blessed are the peacemakers, for they will be called children of God."

Romans 12:18 tells us, "If it is possible, as far as it depends on you, live at peace with everyone." As a child of God, you can bridge the gap when people are arguing with one another. You know the Prince of Peace (Isaiah 9:6), and your job is to introduce him to everyone who will listen. Proverbs 14:30 says, "A heart at peace gives life to the body, but envy rots the bones."

You have the privilege of being led by the Spirit of God. Romans 8:14 says, "For those who are led by the Spirit of God are the children of God."

When Jesus was talking to the people about what it would be like to acknowledge him before men, he said, "When you are brought before synagogues, rulers and authorities, do not worry about how you will defend yourselves or what you will say, for the Holy Spirit will teach you at that time what you should say" (Luke 12:11–12).

When Jesus told his disciples that he would be leaving them, they were confused and despairing. But Jesus told them, "And I will ask the Father, and he will give you another advocate to help you and be with you forever—the Spirit of truth. The world cannot accept him, because it neither sees him nor knows him. But you know him, for he lives with you and will be in you" (John 14:16–17).

You have the very Spirit of the living God within you to lead you and guide you into all truth.

You have the privilege of sharing in Christ's glory as you share in his suffering. Romans 8:16–18 says, "The Spirit himself testifies with our spirit that we are God's children. Now if we are children, then we are heirs—heirs of God and co-heirs with Christ, if indeed we share in his sufferings in order that we may also share in his glory. I consider that our present sufferings are not worth comparing with the glory that will be revealed in us."

As a child of God, you will inherit eternal life with Jesus. He has gone to prepare that place in glory for you (John 14:2).

You have the privilege of being clothed with Christ. Galatians 3:26–27 tells us, "So in Christ Jesus you are all children of God through faith, for all of you who were baptized into Christ have clothed yourselves with Christ."

All the qualities that Christ possessed—humility, gentleness, patience, goodness, and much more—are now covering you. Jesus is your garment. He protects you, he displays his glory through you, and he covers you in peace.

You have the privilege of being a minister of reconciliation. Second Corinthians 5:18–20 says, "All this is from God, who reconciled us to himself through Christ and gave us the ministry of reconciliation: that God was reconciling the world to himself in Christ, not counting people's sins against them. And he has committed to us the message of reconciliation. We are therefore Christ's ambassadors, as though God were making his appeal through us. We implore you on Christ's behalf: Be reconciled to God."

Just as you were brought into God's kingdom, you have the right and the privilege of helping others see that Jesus Christ paid the penalty for their sins so they could be reconciled to God.

Have you fully embraced your identity as a child of God? Is that the first thing that comes to mind when you think about who you are? Find some time today to meditate on the verses above and ask God to make them a part of your self-identity.

Release Who You Thought You Were

Take a deep breath or two. If tears hover, let them come. Picture a child who has lived as an orphan or within an abusive family, but who now stands before a judge to become a full-fledged member, a beloved child, of a forever family.

Adoption is not something anyone takes lightly. Especially God. When he says that you are now his child through faith and by the blood of Jesus, then that's what you are, forever. Nothing you can ever do or say can separate you from his love.

Hold out your hand to symbolize taking the hand of your heavenly Father. When insecurity and the wounds of your past seek to wrench your hand out of his, remember that the one who is in you is greater than the one who is in the world (1 John 4:4). Nothing can snatch you out of God's hands.

There's an old classic Disney movie called *The Apple Dumpling Gang*. Three orphans in the Old West are sent to live with an unknown uncle after their parents pass away. When they arrive, the uncle is nowhere to be found, but there is a ramshackle cabin that apparently used to be his. They are poorer than poor until they discover a huge gold nugget in a mine that belonged to their father, and, by virtue of being his children, that nugget now belongs to them.

A man and his new wife who have been taking care of the children and fallen in love with them file papers to adopt the children. But before papers can be signed, would-be parents come out of the woodwork. Spoiler alert: All of them prove false, and the children go home with the ones who truly love them.[4]

Don't let Satan tell you that you belong to anyone else but your heavenly Father. You were bought at a price (1 Corinthians 6:20), and you belong to his family forever.

Father, being your child is almost too much for me to understand. Help me grasp fully that you have adopted me. You have set me free from my bondage to sin. Let me live free as your beloved child so your love will overflow from me into those around me. Just as you sent your Son into the world, so send me into the world, in the power of your Holy Spirit, as a minister of reconciliation and an ambassador for your kingdom. What a privilege that is! It's in the precious name of Jesus that I pray, amen.

JOURNAL PROMPT: Make three lists. Who does the world say you are? Who do you say you are? Who does God say you are?

NOTES

Introduction
1. "Facts and Statistics," Anxiety and Depression Association of America, https://adaa.org/understanding-anxiety /facts-statistics.
2. Anjel Vahratian et al., "Symptoms of Anxiety or Depressive Disorder and Use of Mental Health Care Among Adults During the COVID-19 Pandemic — United States, August 2020–February 2021," *Morbidity and Mortality Weekly Report* 70, no. 13 (April 2021): 490–94, http://dx.doi.org /10.15585/mmwr.mm7013e2.
3. Judy Johnson, "These Are 10 of the Most Googled Mental Health Questions—And We've Got the Answers," Get the Gloss: Expert Health and Beauty, July 26, 2019, https://www.getthegloss.com/article/the -most-googled-mental-health-questions-answered.

Part 2: Lies
1. Simon Burton, "50 Stunning Olympic Moments No. 3: Derek Redmond and Dad Finish 400m," *Guardian*, November 30, 2011, https://www.theguardian.com/sport /blog/2011/nov/30/50-stunning-olympic-moments-derek -redmond.

2. *Cast Away*, directed by Robert Zemeckis, starring Tom Hanks and Helen Hunt (Los Angeles, CA: 20th Century Fox, 2000).

Part 3: Fear

1. Katherine James, *A Prayer for Orion: A Son's Addiction and a Mother's Love* (Downers Grove, IL: InterVarsity Press, 2020), 145–46.
2. David Guzik, "Psalm 56: Faith in the Midst of Fear," Enduring Word, 2020, accessed August 10, 2021, https://enduringword.com/bible-commentary/psalm-56/.

Part 4: Loneliness

1. Mayo Clinic Staff, "Stress Relief from Laughter? It's No Joke," Mayo Clinic, accessed August 10, 2021, https://www.mayoclinic.org/healthy-lifestyle/stress-management/in-depth/stress-relief/art-20044456.
2. "Brain Training and Dementia," Alzheimer's Society, accessed August 10, 2021, https://www.alzheimers.org.uk/about-dementia/risk-factors-and-prevention/brain-training.

Part 5: Everyday Concerns

1. "Stress in America: Paying with Our Health," American Psychological Association, February 4, 2015, https://www.apa.org/news/press/releases/stress/2014/stress-report.pdf.
2. "George Müller: Trusting God with Daily Bread," Harvest Ministry, accessed August 10, 2021, http://harvestministry.org/muller.
3. "The Drowning Man," TruthBook, accessed August 10, 2021, https://truthbook.com/stories/funny-god/the-drowning-man.
4. "Workplace Stress," American Institute of Stress, accessed August 10, 2021, https://www.stress.org/workplace-stress.

5. "What Does James 1:17 Mean?" Got Questions Ministries, n.d., https://www.bibleref.com/James/1/James-1-17.html.

Part 6: Shame

1. Diane Shirlaw-Ferreira, "What Does It Mean to Be Holy and Blameless in the Bible?," *Worth beyond Rubies* (blog), July 18, 2021, www.worthbeyondrubies.com/holy-and-blameless.
2. Anna I. Smith, "The Crippling Effects of Shame," *Assemblage* (blog), Medium, March 10, 2020, medium.com /assemblage/the-crippling-effects-of-shame-64a4f7d649e.
3. "The Legacy of Chuck Colson," Prison Fellowship, accessed August 10, 2021, https://www.prisonfellowship.org/about /chuck-colson/.
4. "About Nicky Cruz," Nicky Cruz Outreach, accessed August 10, 2021, https://nickycruz.org/about/.

Part 7: Anger

1. Ross Cavitt, "Woman Finds Strangers Living in Home, and Now She Can't Get Them Out," WSB-TV online, Cox Media Group, July 5, 2017, www.wsbtv.com/news/local /cobb-county/woman-finds-strangers-living-in-home-and -now-she-cant-get-them-out/550775721/.
2. "The Count of Monte Cristo Summary," LitCharts, accessed August 10, 2021, https://www.litcharts.com/lit /the-count-of-monte-cristo/summary.
3. Jennifer Breheny Wallace, "Why Getting Even May Make You Feel Worse in the Long Run," *Washington Post*, November 11, 2017, https://www.washingtonpost .com/national/health-science/why-getting-even-may -make-you-feel-worse-in-the-long-run/2017/11/10 /a314d54e-b440-11e7-9e58-e6288544af98_story .html?utm_term=.14a1bc29a25e.

4. Catiana Nak Kheiyn, "What Does It Mean to 'Heap Burning Coals' on Your Enemy's Head?", 412Teens.org, June 2021, https://412teens.org/qna/what-does-it-mean-to-heap-burning-coals-on-your-enemys-head.php.

5. "Forgiveness: Your Health Depends on It," Johns Hopkins Medicine, accessed August 10, 2021, https://www.hopkinsmedicine.org/health/wellness-and-prevention/forgiveness-your-health-depends-on-it.

6. "Forgiving Yourself," AllAboutGod.com, accessed August 10, 2021, https://www.allaboutgod.com/forgiving-yourself.htm.

Part 8: Identity

1. Britannica, s.v. "Symphony No. 9 in D Minor, Op. 125," last modified February 21, 2019, https://www.britannica.com/topic/Symphony-No-9-in-D-Minor.

2. Rick Renner, "The Applause of God," Renner.org, accessed August 10, 2021, https://renner.org/article/the-applause-of-god/, italics in original.

3. Kathleen Kaiser Harl and Tim Pitcher, "Why Did God Create Me Like This?," Cru, accessed August 10, 2021, https://www.cru.org/us/en/communities/athletes/why-did-god-create-me-like-this.html.

4. Disney Fandom, s.v. "The Apple Dumpling Gang," accessed August 10, 2021, https://disney.fandom.com/wiki/The_Apple_Dumpling_Gang.

Welcome to Abide.

We'll meet you right where you are.

Find daily inspiration

Overcome life's challenges

Calm your mind with God's peace

Be well with us.

Abide is a Christian wellness app designed to help you stress less and sleep better through guided, Bible-based meditations, bedtime stories, breathing exercises, and more.

Download Abide today to start your wellness journey and access our library of over 2,000 pieces of content, with new meditations added daily.

Peace with the Psalms

40 Readings to Relax Your Mind and Calm Your Heart

Devotions from Abide Christian Meditation

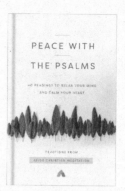

We live in a busy world; from work and family obligations to friendships and faith, daily life can sometimes make us dizzy with stress or overcome with worry. And though many of us try to slow down, it can be difficult to calm our minds and tune our hearts into the messages that matter most.

But the good news is that peace and comfort are attainable, even when your heart is at its most restless. In *Peace with the Psalms*, authors from Abide Christian Meditation—the world's most popular Christian meditation app—lead you through the best of the psalms so you can find peace and renewal in God's promises.

In each of 40 carefully crafted biblical meditations that include Scripture, a guided reflection, and a prayer, you will learn to:

- Shift your focus from today's circumstances to the promises of God
- Experience the principle of patience, reassuring believers in the darkest times
- Find rest by memorizing and repeating key verses and passages
- Overcome the common resistance to joy that comes from overactivity
- Engage your senses in imagining the word pictures of the Psalms

No matter what you're going through, *Peace with the Psalms* offers comfort from God's Word. By reflecting on the biblical messages in these pages, you'll remember each day that God is near.

Available in stores and online!